Our Pink Depot
The Gay Underground FLO-N202-236000000-TRK-MST-00002-SAY-HELLO-WAVE-GOODBYE-KEN-NIE-BPS

Nina Wakeford

Art on the Underground Book Works

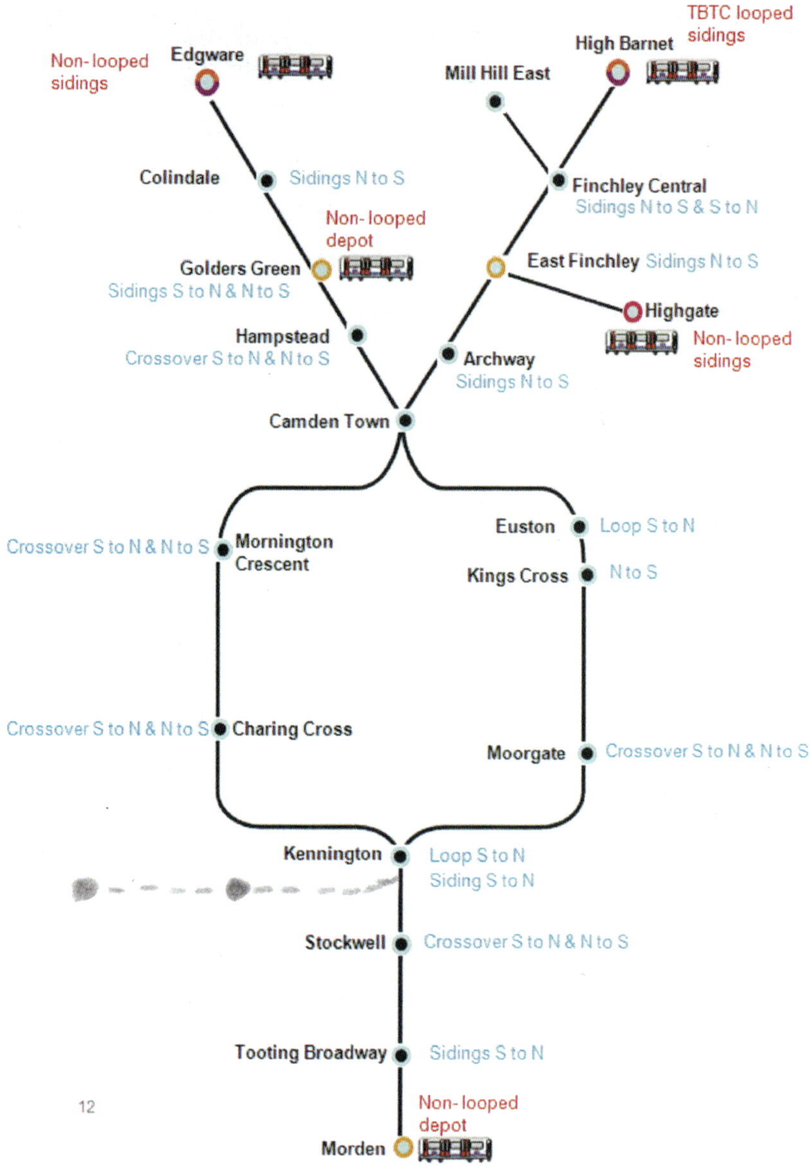
Non-looped sidings
Edgware
TBTC looped sidings
High Barnet
Mill Hill East
Colindale
Sidings N to S
Finchley Central
Sidings N to S & S to N
Non-looped depot
Golders Green
Sidings S to N & N to S
East Finchley
Sidings N to S
Highgate
Non-looped sidings
Hampstead
Crossover S to N & N to S
Archway
Sidings N to S
Camden Town
Euston
Loop S to N
Crossover S to N & N to S
Mornington Crescent
Kings Cross
N to S
Crossover S to N & N to S
Charing Cross
Moorgate
Crossover S to N & N to S
Kennington
Loop S to N
Siding S to N
Stockwell
Crossover S to N & N to S
Tooting Broadway
Sidings S to N
Non-looped depot
Morden

Northern Line walking times

Location	From	To	Minutes
High Barnet	Booking On Point	Sidings	**7**
Finchley Central	Platform	25 Siding*	**4**
		26 Siding*	**3**
East Finchley	Booking On Point	Highgate Sidings	**19**
	Booking On Point	Highgate Sdg (North end)	**16 +**
	Highgate Sidings (Northend Roads)	Booking on Point	**16 #**
Archway	Platform	Siding*	**3**
Edgware	Booking On Point	North Siding	**5**
		16 Siding*	**4**
		South Siding	**9**
Colindale	Platform	Siding*	**2**
Golders Green	Booking On Point	Depot	**7**
		24, 25 siding and loop*	**5**
		26 Road*	**7**
	Depot	Depot Exit (Finishing Duty)	**6**
	26 Road	Depot Exit (Finishing Duty)	**6**
Euston	Station Sup Office	Loop*	**4**
Kennington	Platform	Siding*	**5**
Tooting Broadway	Platform	Siding*	**3**
Morden	Booking On Point	Depot (Northend Roads)	**12 ****
	Booking On Point	Depot (All other Roads)	**15**
	Depot	**Depot Exit (Finishing Duty)**	**7**

replaced the ground with slotted concrete rings, forming a space through which passenger trains will run, soon. Mark shared stories about miners who were brought down from the North, tunnelling with hand tools in spaces these machines could not reach. We spoke of the alliances in the 1980s over pit closures and Clause 28, and the cultures of mines and nightclubs and politics, back then.

850,000 tons of 'muck' were extracted from here to enable the extension of the Northern line. On the trackwalk we occupied the tunnels with our bodies and our words, spoken and sung.

At tunnel ring 980 we paused to hear the Victoria line trains, two metres above us.

At the first cross passage between the northbound and southbound tunnels we stopped as Nina spoke the words of gay DJs from the Market Tavern, a demolished pub which had stood above us at 1 Nine Elms Lane and had been frequented by the Flower Market porters from 5am. She also sang.

At Nine Elms station, she proposed that these tunnels would be our new pink depot.

At the Battersea crossover box, we remembered all those Underground staff who died from HIV and AIDS, scattering red ribbons amongst the concrete dust.

We undertook our trip shortly before they closed the final mole hole from the tunnels to the sky, so at Battersea we looked up and saw the night, eight levels above us.

> 'The drivers who walked with us were all lesbian or gay.
> These tunnels have been our workplace,
> and soon the tunnels will be theirs.'

With thanks to the six operatives from **Golders Green** and **Morden**.

Above this new tunnel the MARKET TAVERN once stood. Grey concrete outside. Cherry red, dark, sexy, cruisy inside.

At the Flower Market, all our conversations happened before five am. After that, the nightmen setting up the show had gone home, and the salesmen were too busy to talk.

He said: Yeah, 1970s.

Yeah, the Market Tavern was one of those things you either got bitten by it, or you just could just pop in... on your way home.

Well I'd go up there at five o'clock. Cos I didn't drive then. I couldn't get home. So I'd go up there. But then it just became life, that you didn't go home. I'd be up there five til nine every single day. Then I'd go home. It wasn't really fair to my family.

On an average morning, twenty to thirty regulars. And then the daymen used to just drift up there, and then pop up for a whiskey-coffee and then go back down.

It was a mezzanine, connecting two towers. It was in the Market Towers. The bar was very dark, cos there were no windows out onto the street. So it was dark in there.

There was two entrances. One across the mezzanine where the porters used to go in, to our bar. And the stairs where that photo was taken used to go up to the bigger bar.

It was owned by quite a lot of people. The one I know was a Turk. He was also involved with Crystal Palace.

That bar, a lot of croupiers used to go in there. A lot of police used to go in there. But they wasn't allowed in the Market bar. So they used to pay the normal price, whereas the market porters paid a subsidised price.

There was a door between, into the toilets.

Yeah, we had shared toilets. But we didn't want to mix with them. The last thing you wanted to do was be sitting there with police. Completely two ends of the spectrum, isn't it? I mean, you've got the workers, and you've got the policemen.

On a Saturday it was fantastic up there, cos you used to get the airline pilots come in. And they liked to play pool. And I've seen games of pool for a thousand pounds. But you can imagine what a thousand pounds to a porter was, when his wage was only a hundred and eighty pounds a week.

If you had a day off, or if you went on holiday, you'd come back and your first thing... right what's been happening? And they'd say, oh, you missed it!

Something was always… it was a hive of activity there. You know what I mean? It was such a buzz.

I started work in May 1975. The Market opened in November 1974. And I became a member of the pitching in gang. There were fourteen of us, working in pairs.

Buster Edwards, Great Train Robbery, up the Market Tavern every single day. Ever seen the film *Buster*?

We knew he didn't want to talk about it.

Roy Steptoe

John Conteh

> He said: You used to get the overflow from the West End. They would be there at five o'clock in the morning. So you would have characters who had been out in the West End in the other bar as well.
>
> Probably Thursday. Thursday or Friday we would have gone in there to have a drink after work. When I was eighteen, twenty, I'd have gone probably Thursday, Friday. But then the Podium restaurant opened, round the corner. And that took a lot of people away. That was a lot nicer.
>
> Yeah, yeah. From the Market Towers they all used to come down. All these office girls and that, so they would all be down there for lunch, so people started going around there. That's probably why the Market Tavern closed in the end. Although it went, obviously it went gay.
>
> I'd have thought in the 1980s. I was probably twenty odd.
>
> Yes, I'd say early 1980s.
>
> Oh yeah. All of a sudden it turned. I suppose the overflow of the West End turned into the gay scene, coming down there. And then there were more gays. And then eventually there was a lot of gays there in the public bar. And then I suppose it took over.
>
> Together there, yeah. In the 1980s.
>
> We would have still mostly stayed in the Market bar. They would have been round the other bar.

The first time I went there, I was about, I'd have been fourteen. I was a tea boy. I was a tea boy in the old Market, which was WC1, from 1969. And the Market moved in 1974. Yeah, fourteen.

Yeah, yeah, I'd have been fourteen. I weren't drinking. I weren't drinking alcohol. But I used to go there because everyone I worked for used to go in there drinking. I started drinking when I was sixteen.

Oh, the last time I would have been probably twenty-five. So 1986.

It was a dingy hole. The Market bar was very dark, because it had no windows, because you were on the inside. And the main bar had windows, that was quite light and quite nice. Looking back towards where the Flower Market would have been. But the Market bar had no windows, and it had pool table.

That was the smaller bar, yeah.

I would say it was motley wall paper. Dark reds. It had leather, I know it had leather benches. But in the Market bar it was quite dark. Always was.

> He said: I shouldn't think the owner ever had to buy a tomato or a potato or a cucumber, no.
>
> You won't know this, but on a certain day of the week there was what you call a cotchel.
>
> A cotchel is like a bag of potatoes… half filled with potatoes. It would have your weekend vegetables in it. It might even have a packet of eggs in it. And it might even have a small bunch of flowers. But it is what you took home from the market. We would swap our flowers for fruit and veg.
>
> Yeah, cos the guvnors were pretty good, you know. To save you thieving it, they'd say help yourself to a few bunches there. That one's been a bit damaged, take that.
>
> Well you took the extra bunches and ones they didn't know about… and the ones you wanted you kept, obviously. But, then there was a trade. Yeah. So that was someone from the fruit side who had a drink with you, and a trade. And I'll tell you, on a Friday I could say that if seventy-five percent of that stuff got taken home, there would be twenty-five of it left. In the bar.

Eighteen metres below ground, and illuminated by temporary lighting, the Head of Tunnelling whistled one of his favourite songs from his walks in the mines in Yorkshire, years previously. After thirty seconds, his tune was accompanied by the rumble then roar of a Northern line train running round the loop. He kept whistling.

He said: You want me to sing it?

I can't remember the words, hang on.

He sang: *Standing in the door of the Pink Flam-ing-o… cry-ing in the rain... Du du du du… du du du… It was a kind of so-so love… and I'm gon-na-make sure it never happens ag-a-in… Me and thee... it had to be… the standing joke of the year… You were a sleep around… ur, lost and found… and not for me I fear… Du du du du, du du du…* there you go.

I can't remember any more… (starts singing again) *Take a look at my face… for the last time... You never see me… I never saw you… say hello, good-bye… Du du du du… du du du.*

Ha, ha, ha.

I got it from them. A lot of the old mine deputies would do it. They'd come in and they would be singing along. And you'd hear their voices from like, ah, hundreds and hundreds of yards away before you could even see them. Especially on the quiet back return roadways, if the air was blowing the right direction. Yeah, you would pick them up.

Oh, old bloody songs, wouldn't they? All old guys, weren't they?

Oh, gosh. I remember one guy always used to sing *Don't Cry for me Argentina.* But he used to substitute the words. So, for other women. So I think it was…

He sings: *Don't Cry for me Gladys Lum-ber-ton… Because the truth is I nev-er left you… All through my wild days… My mad ex-is-tence… I kept my pro-mise… You kept your dis-tance.*

When I was walking round... once I was a mine deputy and walking round mines doing inspections, yeah I'd always sing. Yeah, that was quite common if you were walking around... bear in mind I could be… there's times when I've been in a whole coal mine which could have fifty, sixty, seventy miles of ventilated tunnels, down a long shaft half a mile deep. I could be down there on my own, you know? And I'm walking around, miles from the shaft, in a big black tunnel, on my own. So the only person who is going to give me any company is myself. And it is quite normal to walk along singing… singing, whistling, humming. *Dum-di-dum-di-dum.* Yeah, course you would. Cos you'd

Standin' at the door of the Pink Fla-

go crazy if you didn't talk to yourself, wouldn't you? I mean twelve hours doing an inspection on a Saturday night when you are on the only one in the mine, that's a long… you'd have a lot of areas to inspect to make sure everything was OK. Yeah, you would ride on the conveyor belts, you'd jump on the locos, yeah you would do all that. But you are still walking a lot.

At Golders Green, a Northern line train depot, we discussed the absence of TfL operatives at Pride 2019, the importance of solidarity on the job, and how the timetable might hinder this. We spoke in the canteen, four hours into the shift, about her voice in the tunnels.

She said: You are not supposed to say ladies and gentlemen when you make your announcements… and I say *supposed* because I don't, um, just because nobody has managed to give me an alternative.

Since… since when? January last year. But they never gave us an alternative.

For equality purposes. To not exclude anybody. Don't use the greeting ladies and gentlemen.

I say ladies and gentlemen.

The thing is because I consider myself a lesbian, and <   >… there are a lot of boxes that I tick. Saying ladies and gentleman is an accepted form of greeting. I do not feel like I'm being excluded or discriminated against.

How far do you go? I didn't go into politics… but how far do you go before you hand it to every individual and the whole gets lost?

If you are in a tunnel, someone has to grab your attention first. If you just start off with an announcement that gives essential information, they are not going to hear the first four or five words.

At Morden depot, we sat in the large room behind the drivers' booking on desk, surrounded by boxes of sturdy black shoes. Every Tube driver can broadcast pre-recorded announcements via the public announcement system. Or they can press a different button in the cab, and speak to the passengers directly.

She said: It's like, yeah, there was something recently about drivers saying hello everyone, or morning, or good afternoon all. I, unfortunately, still say ladies and gentlemen. I actually say ladies and gents.

mingo cryin' in the rain   It was a kind of so-so love   And I'm gonna make sure it doesn't hap-

I still say it, and, you know what, to be fair, I don't even know many people pay attention to it. They just want the information.

It's everyone. Yeah, a hundred per cent.

And, you know what, I think people pick up on your tone, more. And um, I've had my own little things that I say.

Like, if I don't know something, I just tell them I don't know. I'm like, listen, I haven't been given any information. This is a nightmare this morning. I wouldn't blame you if you got off and got on another line. We're letting you down. I'll have a few jokes. Because it is what it is, you know. I'm really, really honest. Probably to a fault. But then I've had a lot of mystery shoppers, and I always get good scores.

Yeah, I really love talking to my passengers, even though they don't talk back to me.

At Golders Green, on the hottest day of July, each time a train stopped on the platform, we paused for him to check on the driver. For less than two minutes, the cabs stood opposite the door of the Train Manager's office. He offered each driver an ice lolly that he had bought in bulk from Tesco that morning.

He said: I was always making my own PAs, cos obviously I'd done stations so I had no problem using the PA. I was always using the PA and talking to the customers and getting a laugh. My usual thing was at London Bridge… it would be five o'clock because I usually did lates… so I was always a dead late driver at East Finchley and I would open the doors… and I'd be coming through London Bridge and everyone would be looking so upset, and I'd just started saying… now these were the days you could say ladies and gents, so I said now come on ladies and gentlemen, *I've* only just started work and I am smiling. And I still have to work all evening, and you are going home. Now come on, give me a smile. And you would get the odd people laughing, and chuckling and stuff like that. And you would have that kind of bravado.

I'm a big talker, as you can see. I'm not shy in any way, shape or form. I thought I'd get really bored. And you know what, I really enjoyed driving, I really did. And I think it was just I kind of did it as a station by station thing instead of thinking oh I've got eight hours of driving, or anything like that.

And in the southbound running tunnel of the Northern Line Extension we measured the properties of the sound by inflating a balloon, bursting it with a pin, and recording the bang, bodies frozen so as not to interfere. Later, an expert in acoustic metrics emailed his analysis.

From: <   >

The sound is AMAZING! It's highly reverberant at low frequency, as is to be expected for a concrete construction. The RT was 29 seconds at 65 Hz, it gets a bit better at mid and high frequencies, but it's certainly a very lively space. (Look at the T30 metrics.)

and found and not for me, I feel   Take your hands off me, hey   I don't belong to you, you

In this reverberant space we begin the announcements for the new tunnels, for our pink depot.

see And take a look in my face, for the last time I never knew you, you never knew me Say

Ladies and Gentlemen!
All of a sudden it turned. The overflow of the West End turned into the gay scene, coming down there and then there were more gays, and then eventually, there was a lot of gays there in the public bar.

We talked about the jigsaw of venues in Vauxhall and Nine Elms, years ago. Each had its own character, and clientele. And there were stories of staggering back and forth between places on Sundays, from lunchtime until late.

He said: The entry was to the side of it, but in front of it was a big office block, and then The Colosseum, with a walkway from the Market to the Market Tavern. Hence why it is called the Market Tavern. And to gain entry you went up these, like, concrete steps which went up and then took it up, up, straight, and then to the right and a little left up to the doorway. With a great big neon sign which said Market Tavern on it.

It was like a concrete prefab, as us oldies would say.

Inside, well, the bits I can remember of it was a bit dated and tatty. There were really old radiators, and it was really dimly lit, and dark in colour.

I always remember going in there and the toilets were flooded and the water would come down flooding down those stairs and you would be wading in water, tacky dancefloor. The toilets were a mess, but I think it was what we would have called in those days underground gay clubbing, LGBT clubbing. I mean, you didn't mind what the architecture looked like, you didn't mind what your surroundings looked like, you were just there with friends and having a good time.

It was just sad watching it as it was being demolished. I'm sure there's pictures somewhere, possibly I have one going by on a bus where all that was left of it was those concrete steps up to… with nothing else there. I think that the last bit that they demolished was the steps up to it.

The last time I went there was… it went through a bit of a rough time towards the end. The owner of it… had a bit of, what do you call it, dementia. And lost all the licenses. Not lost them by the police or the council. But just forgot to renew them. And a friend of mine… well not particularly a friend now, they decided to break in and reopen it again. But it didn't have any licence and so it was closed down a couple of weeks later.

Probably… let me think, fifteen years ago. And then after it closed down officially, full stop, squatters moved in. And destroyed the place. And I went to have a look with < > and < > and < >. And if it wasn't for the three of them I wouldn't be here today. I was thrown in the deep end where I work, and they kind of gave me lots of advice on how to run pubs, how to clean lines and just how to do general pub jobs.

And it was actually quite soul destroying to go in and see the squatters had destroyed it. There was running water everywhere. The toilets had been taken out, and whether it was the squatters or other people going in, all the pipes were taken out. Whether they were copper, or lead, I don't know. It was trashed, it was really trashed. Whether they were evicted I really can't remember, or if they moved out, but they left the place in a state. Yeah, so it was quite hard to see that part of it.

Usually by the time I got there, I couldn't remember much. When you arrived at the front door you were just so excited to get in. You wanted off the street. You wanted in. There was always a great welcome. Made you feel at home, going in. And that was when I just moved to London.

I can't remember what the night was at that time, but more a kind of underground, the start of the Ecstasy… probably the end of LSD.

It was just dance music. In those days it was hard house.

No, I don't. No.

That's when drugs were good, in those days. It was always a friendly environment, always.

I would have been twenty-five at the time. So it was all new to me. It was underground. It just felt underground. Even though it was legal, it gave the impression that what you were doing was illegal. I mean doing drugs *was* illegal. It still is. But I suppose… because being gay… it was still in those days that even though you knew it was a gay venue, on a Sunday, you still… well, before my time the reason the Market Tavern got its licence was for the Flower Market, so of course when they finished work in the Market they wanted places to drink. And that is the only place in South London that got the license it did. I wouldn't say it was twenty-four-hour, but it was able to open up early in the morning, and I think that's how < >, bless his soul, got away with it, really.

I think it was because we all, us gays all looked after each other. It was a community. It is where you went… it was probably just as mobile phones were coming in… so you would go on a Sunday, if somebody wasn't there, you got worried. Because you would see them on a regular basis, and that is the way it was. It was like going to church.

skirt And me in a suit but it just wasn't me You're used [beat] [beat] [beat] [beat] [beat]

Yeah, like going to church. You looked forward to going, and you made friends there. It was just so friendly. And if you were a new face, and OK I went with friends the first time, but I got to know so many people. And the next thing you are like going every Sunday.

Well, all the bars in Soho had eleven o'clock licenses. The Royal Vauxhall Tavern, Market Tavern, Dukes in Vauxhall, they had what they called a food license, where, believe it or not, you had to serve food. To get your two am licence.

It was more middle aged, when I say middle aged, I mean probably thirty plus.

The Nine Elms Cold Store was still empty, so you used to go to the Market Tavern and cruise there. And then when the Market Tavern would close you would go Rotherhithe to The Orange.

The Cold Store was an old cold store. It is where St George's Wharf's built now. At that age I was a bit too scared to go in. I'd heard all these stories about people falling through the rotting floors and never being seen again.

Oh yeah, a woman who was mother to everybody. She used to have a patty van that was always outside on a Sunday. I think it was there Friday, Saturday, and Sunday as well. But she was a mother to everybody. I just remember her big deep voice and shouting patt-eee. Like that. And she always looked after people who were probably a little worse for wear. And for some odd reason you would go and order a patty and she would have all your problems within five minutes and try and sort them out for you. You enjoyed seeing her smiley face as you were coming out.

Yeah, patties. You know the Jamaican patties that you get. Yeah, yeah, yeah. She was from Jamaica. And she was really sweet and sometimes you did come out a little worse for wear. She'd make sure you got a patty and made sure you knew which direction you were going, left or right to get home. But she seemed to know everybody, and so in those days did the taxi drivers. Particularly the same taxi drivers who knew you were going to Rotherhithe, or elsewhere.

So… yeah, it was one of those things. I think you really had to be there.

One of the bar staff regularly put on *Best of Queen* as he started his shift, and the partying began. He remembered other tunes that filled the dancefloor, and more.

He said: I have a very strong memory of being on the bar, on the front bar, which was unusual for me. I usually manned the back bar. And hearing a song by that band I mentioned earlier, called Snap!

[beat] [beat] [beat] [beat] [beat] [beat] [beat] [beat] [beat]   Mama, just killed a man   Put a

'I've Got The Power'… and just seeing a very, very handsome man, dancing by himself. And watching him. And that was… is just one of those crystal clear memories that you, that you have. Um, but I don't think that song was in any way particularly played. That's probably why I mentioned them when you were asking me about songs. It was a perfect moment.

Yeah, well there wasn't a huge number of people. We normally only had one member of staff on. Early mornings was usually either one woman who often did looking after the back door… who was a trans woman. Or another woman, who was a friend of <   >'s. But it was just one person. And only, what was called our back bar, so our smaller bar, which had lots of fruit machines in it. The sort of predecessors of whatever they call these awful fruit machines now. Fixed, fixed…

Yeah, fixed odd machines.

I don't understand them. But they took a lot of money, unfortunately, from the traders.

They were regular. They were a very, very regular, hard core group. As I said, I don't think it was, I don't think a huge group of people. And I don't think the main income came from the bar, particularly, I think it came from the fruit machines.

So not great for the families of the traders, unfortunately.

Probably overall only ten bar staff. Some who only did the door. Cleaning staff, one. One Ghanaian man, who used to sleep on a shelf in a room for the first few hours of Sunday, and then clean the whole place.

I did see Freddie Mercury there once. And this is something for you to research on YouTube... I think he is wearing a Market Tavern vest in one of their videos.

So it was a black vest and it would have had a little white logo… here. And it would say Market Tavern and I think have a torso of a muscly man.

gun against his head I've got the power I've got the power Like the crack of the

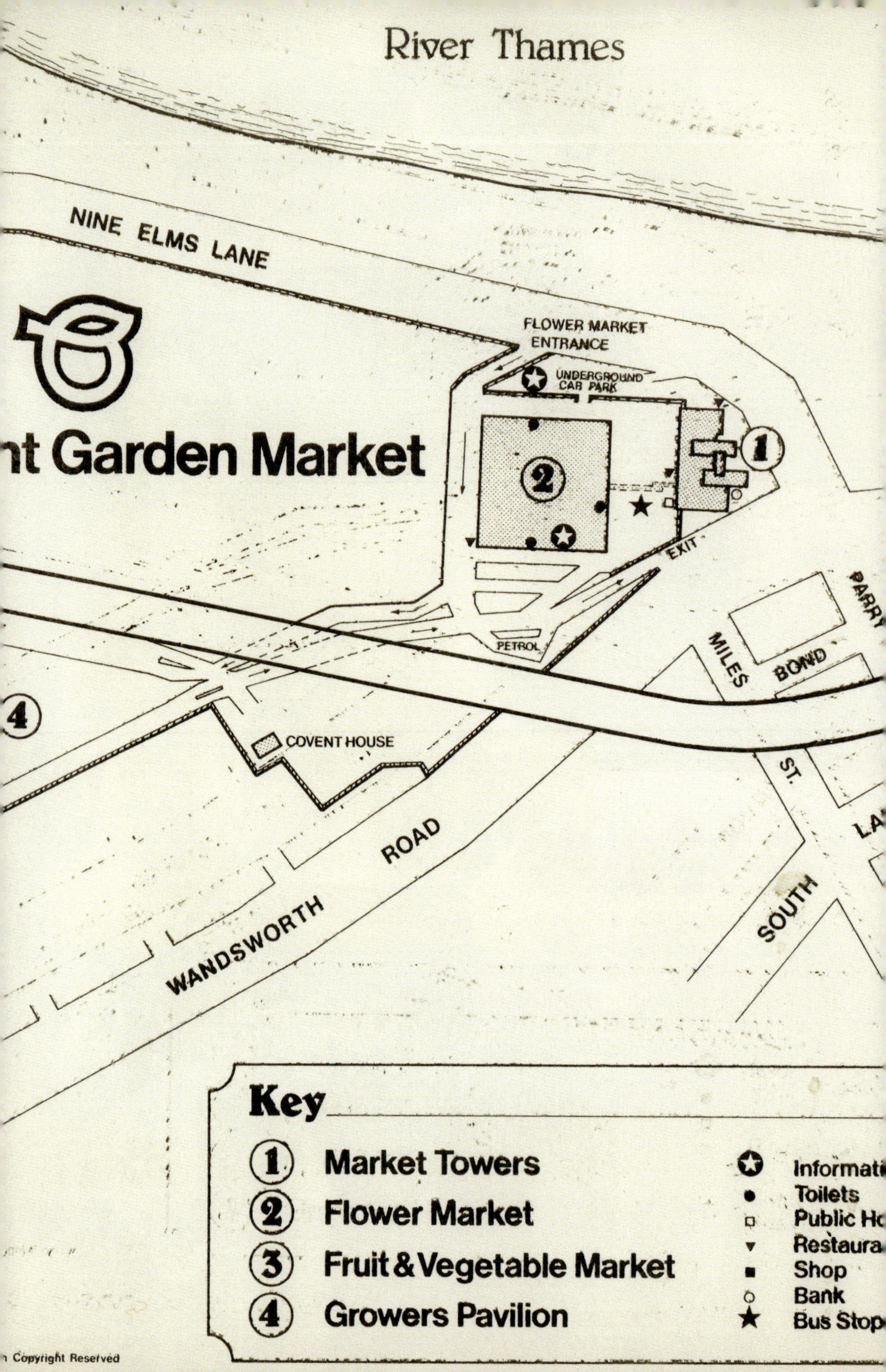
River Thames
NINE ELMS LANE
nt Garden Market
FLOWER MARKET ENTRANCE
UNDERGROUND CAR PARK
EXIT
PETROL
COVENT HOUSE
MILES
BOND
PARRY
ST.
SOUTH
LA
WANDSWORTH
ROAD
Key
1 Market Towers
2 Flower Market
3 Fruit & Vegetable Market
4 Growers Pavilion
Informati
Toilets
Public Ho
Restaura
Shop
Bank
Bus Stop

Ladies and Gentlemen!
After it closed down officially, full stop, squatters moved in. And destroyed the place. All the pipes were taken out. Whether they were copper, or lead, I don't know. It was trashed, it was really trashed.

DESCRIPTION OF PPE	REQUIRED YES / NO	STATE TYPE
HEAD PROTECTION	YES	Helmet EN 397-2012
HEARING PROTECTION	YES	Earplugs/Defenders - TASK
EYE PROTECTION	YES	BS EN 166 , goggles for grout
HIGH VISIBILITY JACKET	YES	(Orange) as per EN 471
HIGH VISIBILTY TROUSERS	YES	(Orange) as per EN 471
RESPIRATORY PROTECTION	YES	Dust Mask – FFP3 –
FOOT PROTECTION	YES	EN ISO 20345:2011: **S3 SRC CI HRO,** wellies for grout
HAND PROTECTION	YES	BS EN 388, gloves for grout
REBREATHER	NO	MSA
OTHER		Protective disposable suits for concreting works

Due to the sound of the tools and machinery, much of our conversation had to be repeated.

She said: OK, at the moment we are in the Northern Line Extension. We are at the first cross passage, eh, of the project.

Well we are just in the tunnel which was made with the TBM [Tunnel Boring Machine], so we are covered with lots of plates. And at the moment the workers are working installing the track. So it doesn't look too messy.

We spoke in the Morden depot about her experiences of being not straight, nor white, nor male, and her curiosity about the new line which she would be driving soon. On the Historic Trackwalk she chose 'Ghetto Heaven' by Family Stand and 'Lifted' by Lighthouse Family.

She said: Yes, so we've got our own little collective, because most people who are gay know that I'm a lesbian. So that is fine. We have our own little thing. A lot of the older drivers I don't think know that I'm lesbian. I think the guy that booked on just before, he has no idea. But I don't care. I really don't.

whip, I Snap attack   Front   You know I love my baby   My baby loves me   My day, it gets

She said: Erm, well at the moment we are using one excavator to be able to install the blocks. And a forklift as well, to be able to move the material we are using to be able to build the track. And also get all the rubbish from the works out. And at the moment we are using just a trolley to move the small things through the tunnel.

> She said: Yeah, I feel really comfortable, really OK.
>
> I remember when I first told him. And I think he said he knew.
>
> He said, well, this is cool. And it sort of made it easier to start telling everyone else. But if it came up in conversation. Cos I think a lot of people talk quite openly about their relationships. And then when you don't... I've had the odd person say, OK, so what's your situation?
>
> I just tell them. Yeah. I don't mind. I don't care. They are like oh! OK!
>
> When I worked at Golders for a short spell I absolutely loved it. I was so welcome. It was fantastic, I really enjoyed it.
>
> Yeah, we went out a few times.
>
> Oh, he is the best.
>
> He can dance really well, actually. Yeah, he can dance really well, yeah, yeah.

She said: Er, exactly, exactly.

Here they are getting the rails on top of the blocks. They are fixing the rail little by little, because the rails are ninety-one metres long. And at the moment a worker is placing that one, that last one there and they need to lift it up little by little every fifteen metres or so.

Yeah, the worker who was just fixing the rails with the last one, he was just using an impact gun to be able to fix the bolts, and that is why it was so noisy.

We have here an Ironman.

Ironman.

It's called Ironman, I don't know why.

> She said: She is the reason we have our own toilets. And a toilet key. And, because I think she was the first... cos the toilets were shared

so heavy   I need a little company   It's quarter to eleven; it's time to make some ghetto hea-

before. And they were just disgusting. Oh my goodness. So, I don't know when she started, I don't actually know how long she's been on the job.

And again, people are surprised that she and I talk. Cos she is a dead early person. And they are deemed the most miserable.

Yes. And when you first meet <   >, she probably doesn't seem the most approachable person. But she has a heart of gold. And how we actually got talking is that we were in the depot. And there was a problem with the points, so we were stuck in there. And our trains were side by side. So we just got out and had a chat. And since then, she is one of my like favourite people.

Yeah, yeah, yeah. And I guess again to look at us, we probably didn't think we had anything in common. But we actually have a quite a few things in common.

She said: And it is used to be able to take the rail and move it, at the same time. That's what they are using every fifteen metres, more or less. And as they soon as they get the first part of the rail, they fix it, with some clips. And after that all they need to do is move the Ironman further, and take the rail into position, little by little.

She said: OK, so you come in, so you book on. So basically, when you come into the office, you are greeted by the manager, and you sign on. And when you sign on you are saying you are fit to commence your duties. Then you look at any information that's in the office. Check your drawer and all that good stuff. You asked if anything is going on. They tell you yes or no. And then you kind of… depending on whether you are picking up from the depot, or whether you are just picking up from the platform, um, if you are picking up from the depot you get half an hour… you've got like seven mins to look at all your notices in the office. Then you get yourself ready to walk to the depot, and then once you get there you've got to speak to the shunter, find out where your train is, what road it is on. And once you get on your train you've got to prep your train for service, which means checking your brakes, and signing to say you have done so, and then you bring the train into passenger service. And then if you don't have a depot pick up you literally just wait for the train in the platform, which is what everyone wants.

So, when you get on your train, the person that has just brought the train in should really come to the front of the train and let you know if there is anything wrong. If there is nothing wrong they don't. But that is how it is meant to go, and then you sort of have to put your details in the train. So what I mean is the train number will be there already, the destination should have been set by the driver who brought the train in.

Yeah, that's correct. So, for example, if a train is coming into Morden, at South Wimbledon the driver will set the destination of where it is going cos it will tell you in your duty book. So that should have been already done for you. In some cases it's not. So, just check that everything is correct there. And then you are meant to put... you have to put your employee number in, and your handheld radio number. So, should your train radio not communicate for any reason, they can contact you on your handheld.

You have one with you all the time.

Yes. Own personal number. So when you do book on you are meant to check your radio's working, your battery's... yeah, all that stuff. So, yeah.

So once you have done that, you are ready. And you literally just wait for the, um, sort of timer to go down, and you get what they call your target point, it makes this dur dur dur noise. You make your announcement to say where you are going. Shut your doors. And then you are off. And then the train just takes you wherever you are going.

She said: Yeah, well it is weird because some of them I know them in English. Because the first time I'm seeing that especially big tool was here. And some of them I know the name in Spanish. It's... is like a mix.

For example, erm, I don't know, for example, the jacks, I knew in Spain that that is called, the translation of that is like cat.

Yes, it is called *gato* and the translation in English is cat.

Well you are learning that every day. Cos the first time you want to translate exactly the same it is not working obviously. You are asking for a cat, they are not going to give you a jack.

It was quite funny as well, because you know a spanner? The tool they are using to fix the bolts?

In Spanish the translation is English key.

English key. English key.

llave inglesa

So the first time I was asking for that. And they were saying what do you want? What do you want? English key? English key?

She said: I think for me, once I leave Morden, the next place I really want to be is Kennington.

keeps it by the radio   And listens to the Reverend preach   It's 10:07, and time to get some

Everything for me is about time. So I know it is twenty minutes from Morden to Kennington.

She said: He is just marking the position of where the block needs to go. And after that, some workers, using some jacks, will put it in position.

For the moment the rails are in place, and that side of the rail is already fixed.

Hm-hmm. Exactly, exactly.

685 milimetres. But we have tolerance, around two to three centimetres.

Yeah. Yeah, exactly.

They are already getting ready the works to be able to lift up the track.

He said: You want to speak with me?

He laughed: I only speak in Spanish. I don't speak English.

She said: He is the one in charge of the gun.

The team.

Ah! No, no, no! The *gang*!

She said: Once I understood the culture of the canteen in particular, I kind of got where people were coming from. So you have got a lot of the older staff that have been here, and drove the different stocks, and have been through a lot of changes. And I think, when I first arrived at Morden, they didn't know who I was, and they just thought I was an excited young lady. And you know, you will soon get over this. It gets really boring, and all the rest of it. But once I started to engage with them, and ask them about their experiences, oh my God I broke down so many barriers, and, um, yeah, now I'm friends with like people… people see me talking to all these different people, and are like how do you know her? How do you know him? And I'm like, I don't know, we just spoke. So they'll not talk to you, but if you talk to them... it kind of, you know.

So as you enter, it is Morden drivers to the left and then you've got bus staff and other depots. So High Barnet, East Finchley and Golders, on the right.

Yeah. So when I first came in, I didn't know about this. So I just went and sat on the right. So they all assumed I wasn't a Morden driver. And then… no one told me. Because I guess if you say this out loud it's absurd,

ghetto heaven Ghetto heaven It's time to get some ghetto heaven Ghetto heaven She

isn't it, really? It is just like school! So I sat over on the right, minded my own business, looking at my books, and stuff. And then someone that I knew, sort of came in and said, you are sitting on the wrong side. And I said what do you mean, the wrong side? And he said, no Morden drivers sit over here. And I said, oh, don't pull my leg. This is ridiculous. So I can't sit here? He said you can, but no one, no one will know you are a Morden driver. So I went over to the left, and slowly but surely people started talking to me. And I thought oh my goodness, where are we? So I kind of made it a thing where I just sit where I want. I mean, now that people know me... I just sit where I want.

Yeah, I guess.

I would say at least maybe about a hundred and fifty to talk to.

I just talk to loads of people. Cos I just think it helps your day out. I spend most of my time here. And you learn so much from people, you know?

Cos, a lot of people have come on to this job, and their parents, or their fathers, grandfathers have been on the job. And I like to hear all that. Like once a guy jumped in my cab. And then I found out that his dad was on the Underground and he sort of pointed out all these secret tunnels, as we were going up from Morden. And I was fascinated. And he couldn't believe it. He thought I was pulling his leg. And I said, no, this was fascinating. And I was like you don't get that I'm genuinely interested. And I said, just stay on the train with me. And he said, no I have to get off.

But a lot of them, <   >, he was the most senior guy, always smiling. It was so admirable. I just thought to myself you have been here for forty-five years. And you are still smiling. And he said, I come here for rest. To get away from my wife. And I said stop it!

She said: Now, before that, they are going to put in position... because that mark, we saw before, that mark needs to be in the middle of the block and they try to adjust as much as possible. But now, because the rail is in position now, the beginning of the rail is where it needs to go, er, they are going to use some jacks to lift up the rail a little bit, and lift all the blocks into position.

And as soon as that is gone, they can start, clipping the rails.

That mark is just a sign along the top of the rails, to let everyone know until where we are going to need to lift up the rails to have a section ready for tomorrow.

needs a little ghetto heaven   Baby, baby, baby   All I need in this world is you   And when

She said: I've always followed the roster. Because I feel when you are doing mixed shifts, it makes it easier to swap. There is nothing I particularly like more than anything else. I'd say my worst shifts are the latest.

Yeah, so the latest you can finish on a late is one thirty in the morning. I just find it quite lonely. You know, because your passengers start dropping off. And, you just think it is just you, really. You are picking people up but it is the odd person. And then I just feel like the whole world is sleeping. You are the only one awake. Even though people are awake. But it just feels so lonely. When I clock off I think no one cares if I get home.

Always at Morden. Yeah.

You will have a TM [Trains Manager] on the desk, and your engineering trains going up and down. Cos when you are working lates, when it gets to about twelve thirty and you start driving through and you see all the night staff coming in, sitting on the platforms waiting to start their bits. And you think oh I shouldn't be here, I should be at home. But some people love it.

She said: Exactly. This is the minimum production that we need to do for the day shift.

Since the last pour, we are going to have around seventy-five metres in position. And tomorrow they are going to be pouring sixty, between sixty and sixty-five metres.

Every morning we are doing the handover, eh, the engineers…

Well between half six and half seven, my colleague <   > he is an engineer as well, and…

No, no, no, <   >, working on this.

And as well, a supervisor of the works. We are talking about the production that night, and if we had any problem, or things need to be solved on days. Because on days we have more people working, like fitters or electricians. So if you have any problems on nights, they can solve them first thing in the morning. To avoid delay in the works.

Yeah, around, well around, needs to, we need to wait until eight because before that it is not allowed to make noise, because of the neighbours, they are too close.

So usually we are starting, if everything is OK, about half eight, nine.

Exactly, exactly.

you're gone   Baby, baby, baby   Your touch, your kiss always gets me through   Sister needs

She said: OK, dead earlies... when I was on the station I loved it.

Yeah, yeah, yeah. Because you had no choice but to be awake. You were on your feet. And you know, you are talking to people. On the trains I hate it. Oh my goodness. Yeah, it's so hard, like when I wake up at three something I feel like, like my body's shutting down, honestly, it feels so horrible. And then when you get up and you are here, it is not so bad. But when you get home... so it's really hard. I will do them if I have to, and normally you have two weeks of each shift. By week two, I'm over it. So what I often do is I'll do my first week full of energy, and I'll try it and whatever. Week two I want to cry. Honestly, I'm a big baby when it comes to dead earlies. And then I have to give them away. And there is so many people who will snap them up. I don't know why they love them. Maybe it is because they have children. I don't have children, so.

We have a group where you can post your swaps. The only thing you can't get rid of is the dead lates.

She said: The clips. Yeah. They are taking, yeah, the clips to, to take them, ready.

We have a few electric welds. Here I can show you one. There.

And that can't be on the block. Just to avoid like all the force being in that area.

We don't want it all on the block to avoid tension on the point. Because it is more weak than the rest of the rail.

She said: Yeah it's lovely there, isn't it?

Yes.

It's amazing. It is fascinating. And I really feel like they are really friendly and accommodating, there. I can spend ages up there.

It used to be really bad, where you would have to phone up every minute, to say, what's happening? But now as it is kicking off, they give you a call. And you are really surprised. Oh, thank you. Thank you for letting me know. And it makes all the difference. Because, sometimes you don't know what is happening and you can only assume that they are regulating, or whatever. And that is what you tell your customers. But honestly I like to just tell them exactly what is going on to give them a choice to... whether they want to get off or not. Whatever.

You know what, one of the most intimidating parts was actually calling the controller. I don't know why I found that so... I found it so difficult, cos I thought this is not a phone call. And on stations I was so confident

her sugar To get her through the day She doesn't have the money But always got a way

on the radio. But, um, I guess it was I felt this was even more safety critical than being on the stations. So whatever they say, and because they know what they are communicating to you, you've got to be able to repeat it back quite quickly. So I used to think, have I got everything? Have I relayed the information correctly, and, do I really understand what is being asked of me? Stuff like that. I used to panic. But now I realise it takes as long as it takes. So just because they are in a rush, maybe, you just have to do it at your own pace. Because sometimes they might be asking you to do what is called a stock and crew, which means at a terminus you have to swap trains. So you have to know what train it is that you are swapping with. And sometimes you repeat it back, OK, 232 and you put down the handset and you are thinking was that 323?

Yeah, literally every time you pick up that handset. I mean, unless you have an incredible memory. But I don't. Even before you answer, I now just make sure I'm ready. Cos I've done it before. And I'm like, now I have to call them back.

They are actually really nice. They are a lot more approachable than when I was at the control room initially, with the Pic line staff.

She said: And also, well we have another... at the beginning of the rails and at the end... we have a minimum distance we need to have to let the welders after that to weld the rails. And after that, if there is a problem on the weld, they can repair it.

So they mark one of the rails and as soon as they get the two rails on top of the blocks, with a ruler, like a square ruler, they mark the other rail, taking into account the position of the first one.

So now, for example, because we are in a straight line, it is just the same point.

But when you are on a curve, you are going to have less space between blocks in the internal of the radium, than in the external of the radium, of the curve. So that is why they are always doing it like that, to make sure the blocks are in the same position.

The alignment of the track... that step of the project is quite repetitive.

She said: So when the train pulls in I manage to get all my spiel out of the way before I open the doors. So, I announce we are at Kennington, this-train-terminates-here, please-ensure-you-have-all-your-personal-belongings-with-you-before-leaving-the train, then I tell them to cross over to get the train continuing towards Morden. So once I've done that I repeat three times this-train-terminates-here. But then before I actually come into Kennington I have already set up a broadcast to say leave the

> train. So once I do my spiel, I hang up the handset and then press the broadcast message and it will say attention please leave the train now, and it repeats it twice. And then you will see the odd person get off. And then I shut my doors.

She said: Probably the part more interesting about engineering is when they are lifting the rails up, and that's why we are using some jigs to make sure the width of the track is always the same, and some bolts, to be able to play with the rail.

You need to wait until the concrete is hard enough to hold the track, and after twelve hours or so you are able to remove some parts of the track. And other parts you need to wait for a day, to be able to remove it just to avoid being moved after that.

Yeah, exactly, exactly. We are using also some Diecis in the tunnel, so when the concrete is coming, we are pumping from the surface to the pit bottom, on the Diecis. And after that we are using the Diecis to be able to move the concrete in the tunnel.

And after that we are using another pump in the tunnel.

And we use that concrete line, which we have here, to be able send the concrete exactly where the guys are working.

Ladies and Gentlemen!
On a late I just feel like the whole world is sleeping.
You are the only one awake.

The drivers had a range of reactions when they saw the new tunnels for the first time, after the two metal shutters were finally rolled up and the new structures were visible from the Kennington loop.

She said: They are so fresh and shiny! I mean, when we first… all the drivers were absolutely amazed by it. I mean, that was the talk of the canteen. Oh my God! Have you seen Kennington? And a lot of people were wanting to take their phones out, and then realised, actually, oh, might get in trouble if someone finds out.

I'm sure you can. You are by yourself in the loop, and it is a new thing, and it is work related.

It's amazing. It just looks fantastic. And then, you know like when things start to change, you think, how did that get there? What was there before? I just don't quite understand how they just slotted that there. It is just fascinating. I'm really happy I'm here now, to kind of be a part of it.

I'm so excited. I really am. Because I wasn't really interested in anything train, you know. Before joining the Underground. I literally only took the Tube to go to Oxford Circus, to shop.

We pronounced *cerrojo* [bolt] as the overnight rail gang worked around us, and we laughed.

He said: I remember the first movie I watched in England... English movie… *The World's End*. Five lads going around pubs in their town, and they have an alien invasion and they are all British guys in a town. Ah, kind of funny movie, and this British accent, OK? And sometimes I think, I don't know nothing!

I always say the most complicated word for British people to say is *cerrojo*.

Ha, ha, ha. Yeah... because I have the three, three sounds that is quite complicated for a foreign person. *Ce. Erre*, as *ra*, *re* … and J as a *ja* like *jamón*, or *Jo*, *José*. So these three sounds are the most complicated sounds. So I found a word with the three sounds in the same word.

You can see… <   > is surrounded by three guys, speaking in Spanish. Few, few words in English. And he perfectly know what they need to do on the rail.

baby My baby loves me My day, it gets so heavy I need a little company It's quarter to

Well I mean… not all of us are Spanish.

He is from Portugal. He and his brother are from the Dominican Republic. There is another guy from the Dominican Republic. We call him <   >, in Spanish, of course. We have a guy from Peru, a guy from Venezuela. We have a British guy which is originally from Nigeria, as well.

At Golders Green, in his office, we looked at the short circuiting device which is always carried during inspections, in case the rail is live.

He said: The new line will just be another bit of trackwalk to do. Unless Barnet side does it.

So, many times a year you do like a track inspection. After the last train. Walk up the track looking for things which could cause problems for the traffic in the morning.

Yes that still happens on every line. Here, it is Edgware down to Kennington. Each manager has their own little section, with the Health and Safety Manager, because they come along.

I came on in 1971 when I left school as a railway operator apprentice. I started in Harrow-on-the-Hill signal cabin. My father, who was on the Underground at the time, said try this job.

My father was Polish. And he came over in the War. He started at Golders, I'd say in the early 1960s. He started at the bottom as a railman, and that is where he met my mother. She was working at Leicester Square at the time.

Before I came out all I worried about was my parents. Especially my father. Cos he was working here at the time. And I thought if I become a manager, and they all know I'm gay and my father doesn't...

Now I just camp it up.

I've got memories of my father here, and the team.

Ladies and Gentlemen!
That was the talk of the canteen. Oh my God!
Have you seen Kennington?

'Around the Old Camp Fire' by Foo Foo Lammar was his choice, and the boombox blasted it out on the Historic Trackwalk. The burst of camp suddenly filling the concrete tunnel rings made us all smile.

He said: I still had blonde hair when I started. I have a picture of me somewhere coming out of Elephant and Castle sidings with peroxide blonde hair.

<   > kind of became my first gay friend on the Underground. No, now he is a DRM [Duty Reliability Manager], so he does all the incidents.

We became friends. Well, friends with benefits.

Well he thought I was a policeman. I mean he had a gay driver. And he was a gay guard, obviously, so a royal crew.

So, queen on the front, queen on the back.

I keep bumping into him now as he lives near where I live, so we have screaming matches in Asda. He was coming outside Asda with, um, his boyfriend and the alarms went off, as he walked out. And I went, yeah, I wouldn't trust them as far as I could throw them. And I got a load of abuse. And I can't understand why!

So I stayed at Elephant and Castle as a guard, uh, then become a rostered guard, and then rostered guard trainer, and then guard-motorman. And my original driver, cos you used to be crewed, so I would be rostered with a certain driver all the time. On the LER agreement, which was London Electric Railway, um, we all had running mates, so as soon as a vacancy popped up, you fell into that position.

My old driver was a guy called <   >. And he looked after me and he got me through my motors and whatever else and he used to sit down, on our meal breaks, and he would start asking me about train equipment. And I was like, <   > I don't know, I'm just a dizzy queen... no, I was too in the cupboard then.

Um so, I passed out motorman on the Bakerloo and then become an instructor on the Bakerloo as well. Or road trainer, as they called it.

And, then it went OPO [One Person Operation] and lost my guard. Because I'd had about three or four guards by then. It was about 1989 which is the year I had my really bad one under... I had a kiddy under the train which was horrendous. It still affects me now, and I wouldn't want anybody to ever go through that.

After that, the Company plan sprung up on the horizon.

I was like right, OK, I'm going to end up doing six or seven pipes, er, whereas duties were a lot shorter if we just done tunnel work. So I put in for Parsons Green.

Well I knew it was a gay depot, but Elephant and Castle was pretty gay.

Oh yeah, it had a reputation for a long time, Parsons Green.

It was even referred to as the training school. You'd go up to White City, I mean, the first thing they'd say… is anybody for Parsons Green?… training for Parsons Green? And some poor little bloke at the back would put his hand up. And they'd go ooorrcch, you'll find out about the Parsons Green coupling, then.

Yeah. Shunt from the rear. Yeah.

I think the District was quite flamboyant, and the problem, well I wouldn't say problem, at Parsons Green… people think that it was a hugely gay depot… but most of the straight people were so camp you wouldn't know anyway. And they just did it to wind people up.

I mean there was a guy just retired, a guy called <   >, someone complained about him wearing a flat cap on a train. So he wore a wig. A Tina Turner wig.

Oh yeah, he was straight, yeah.

Oh and you had someone called <   > worked there. And he used to do drag acts at Earl's Court. At one of the gay pubs.

So, it got broadcast at White City by the instructors, saying it was a gay depot, so if you were at another line, you knew it was a gay depot. Uh, there were certain characters there.

<   > used to do drag. But the straight drivers at Parsons Green used to, unclip his… cos he used to have all his drag in suitcases, and they used to unclip his suitcases, he would whistle up to the mess room as he was doing a drag act at Earl's Court, and they would hoof it out the window. So there would be skirts and stillis up the platform, and he'd be swearing up at people.

Yeah! So he would finish on the eastbound and say can you chuck my bag out, and they would just unclip it and hoof it out the window.

It was quite closeted. But there was quite some outrageous gay people, you know. That's how come I knew about Cilla, sorry I mean <   >, sorry. And he eventually become a signalman.

of mine that harmonize together Scallywags in sleeping bags and tent flaps all

Yeah, no, no. I think he is retired now.

Well the Vauxhall Tavern was where the Parsons Green farewell dos were held.

Yeah, and there was one guy, who is still at Earl's Court now, er <   >, he is lovely, he cares about everyone. But all the drivers got him up on the stage and asked him outright if he was gay. In the middle of a gay pub.

Why they all went to the Vauxhall Tavern, I've no idea. But the whole depot went there.

So we got a lot of the gay guards from Parsons Green at Elephant and Castle. And they were in a league of their own. We got in excess of twenty extra guards, and twelve of them were gay.

I mean we had Janice, whose real name was <   >, who sadly just passed away.

It was quite funny, he came from the District line, and everybody nicknamed everybody. <   > then struck up a relationship with his guard. Who was a guy called <   >, who went up to do training at somewhere… but his guard was someone called <   > and he was very large, because <   > liked them big. And <   > was quite a skinny little thing, but he did like big men. So he was called Janice, and his guard was called Big Diane.

They lived with each other as well, so.

I mean I remember running with a guy called <   >. He was a guard. And he was very mumsy towards me.

Older, very camp. And totally in love with his boyfriend, and he would tell me what he was cooking his boyfriend for dinner, and whatever else. And he, er, was running with me one week on earlies, so he said, right, he said, so we are not eating that rubbish in the canteen, I'm going to cook you a proper breakfast. So he went up on to platform, I think it is five, at Baker Street, which is a Met platform, went in there, terrified these Met crews who were sitting there. Cos he just flounced in and started unpacking his bag of cooking.

Yeah. Carried it all. He had like a little shopping bag full, bigger than my one probably… so he cooks me breakfast, and we had this lovely breakfast in the morning. And then I said, <   >, we've got to go and pick up, we're late. And he said, ooh, I've got to wash up first.

So he washes all the plates up. We go down to Baker Street platform nine, which is northbound Bakerloo… go down and there. And there is an Area Manager standing at the train. So he is like, you are five minutes late, where have you been? Five minutes over there was a big do. So I said, I was trying to get down the stairs, but my guard cooked me breakfast, and like, just didn't realise what the time was. Cos you don't want to drop the guard in it.

And he said, right, who is your guard? And I said <   >. And he went, oh. And you could see the Area Manager's face drop. He said, he's one of those District line people, isn't he? And I said yes. And he said, I had a run in with him every day last week. And he went to see <   >, and the next thing I know I see <   > at the leading cab door. So this train has been sitting there for five minutes without moving. And then <   > is there with his arms folded. I mean, he used to call me <   > because of my surname. And he said <   >, you tell him that we had a lovely breakfast. And I said <   > I think he just wants us to move the train? Well, I'm going to have a cup of tea before I move now. So he went upstairs to the mess room and made a cup of tea. And this Area Manager was going red with anger. And <   > just said to him, if you don't do it the District Line way, I'm not doing it any way. Then he just got on the back of the train, put the key in, shut the doors, and went. And this Area Manager is like what's happened to the Bakerloo line?

Well it would be nice if they did something at Battersea. Had some natural light down there.

And fresh air.

Or have a picture of a leather queen somewhere. Ha ha ha.

> He said: When I was at the training school in 1985, I do remember the trainer showing us the tunnel telephone, um, handset that the drivers carried. Each driver would carry like a little wooden box, um, just a little handheld wooden box, with a telephone receiver in it, and two clips, you clipped it onto the tunnel telephone wire. And I do remember the instructor saying most drivers carry it correct like this, just hanging it from his hand, as if you were carrying a briefcase. But on the District line they carry it like this. He kind of held up his forearm with a limp wrist, with the tunnel telephone box over the inside of his elbow, so carrying it like a handbag, halfway down your arm.
>
> It was particularly Parsons Green and to a lesser extent Acton Town.
>
> It was quite an old fashioned macho culture. There was one female driver at Morden, who was great fun to work with.
>
> There were one or two other gay guys there, um, who tended to keep themselves to themselves. One of them was the ex-partner of a driver on the Bakerloo line, and this is my coming out story. I hadn't met an openly gay man until I joined London Underground. And as I was

fire   Where the mushrooms used to grow   And me muscles used to show   Around the old

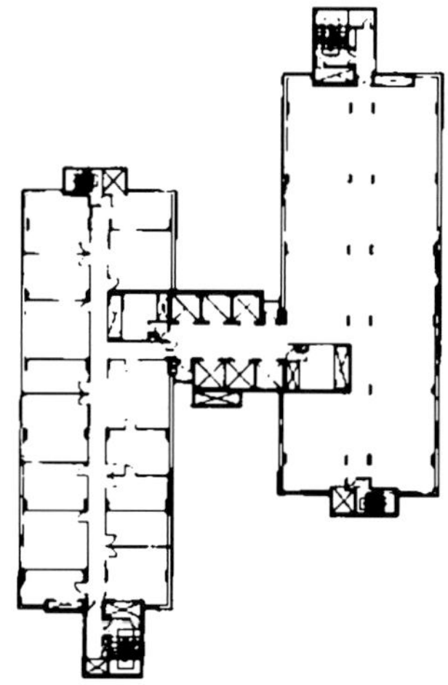

PLAN OF TYPICAL OFFICE FLOOR
Showing Open Plan and Divided Offices

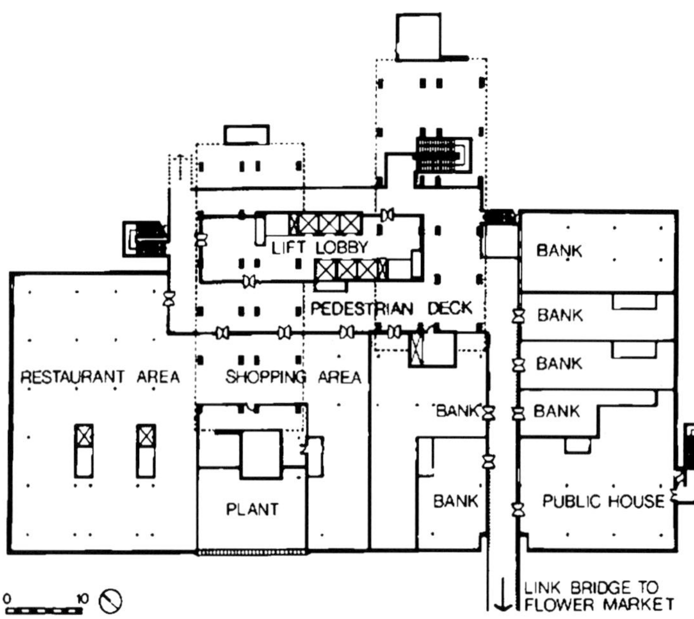

PLAN OF PODIUM LEVEL

The Administration Building, as its name
of the New Covent Garden Market. It
Garden Market Authority and provides
trade associations and other organisations

The Building is situated at the corner c
Road at the apex of the Flower Marke
Flower Market at Podium level. The Podi
and bars and forms the principal circ
become part of the pedestrian high level
Bridge area. Below the Podium are th
situated at ground level to give easy acce
secure corridor leading to the Bank vau
the whole of the Market complex, to
accommodation occupies the two base
177,000 sq.ft. of lettable office space i
height respectively. The plan form of the
central lift lobby and service cores betw
houses six high speed lifts and male and
towers rise 260 ft. and 210 ft. above the
further single floors in the taller block. T
open plan office accommodation.

The construction is of reinforced concret
core and end staircases have insitu rein
vertical strip windows. The concrete has
expose the aggregate. The office towers
with bronze glazing and spandrel panels.

Finishes internally consist of studded rub
walls finished in vinyl wall covering. A
continuous lighting troughs around the p
melamine faced. The toilets are finished
panelled walls and concealed lighting. O
walls and ceilings finished in emulsion pai
whole of the Podium area has studded ru
the external pedestrian areas. The bui
perimeter induction units and the air extr
light fittings.

The boilers, situated in the basement, are
is housed within the Podium level com
provided at 8th and 9th floors and th
building have separate systems served fron

Considerable attention has been paid t
building. A number of semi-mature tr
building and planter boxes have been for
to provide ground cover. Brick paviors to
floor level incorporate the various changes

training on the Bakerloo line, almost without exception my trainer would go, have you met <   > yet? Have you met <   > yet? <   > was quite OTT, um. He had come from the Northern line and he was on the Bakerloo. And he was quite in your face about his sexuality. I think at that point he was a guard, and I think he was actually up at the training school training to be a driver. Anyway, one day I came in for my shift, and there was this character who I hadn't seen before, who was being very in your face, rather camp. And I said to my driver, don't tell me that is <   >. As I understand it, he and his driver were a couple, and whether it was after they split up, I don't know what the story was. We had a common interest. He was a bit of a train anorak and at that point I was an unreformed transport anorak. And he was also good friends with <   >. So think one day we had been to the Science Museum, me, <   > and <   >. And they were going to go to the Union Tavern in Camberwell that night, which was a gay pub, and did I want to come along. And I suppose deep down, I kind of was questioning. But I hadn't said anything to myself at that point. Perhaps I wanted to explore more about my sexual orientation but was too scared to. You know, it was 1985. The only kind of gay men that I was aware of were John Inman or Larry Grayson, that's if he actually was. And I suppose with a lot of talk of gays and poofters and queers and benders at school and actually in depots as well, did I really want to be one of those people?

And I met up with <   > and <   > a couple more times, and I think they took me to the Market Tavern, pretty sure we went to the Vauxhall Tavern.

I'd just moved to Morden at that point as well.

Then when I came back to Elephant and Castle I had truly come out.

Once I came out I started being a bit outrageous, and perhaps gone a bit too far sometimes.

I do remember once being called bummer boy in quite a nasty way by couple of guards at Morden. Um… What could you do about it?

I wasn't aware of any bi people, any trans people, any lesbians on the Northern line when I was there. There was a lesbian on the Jubilee line.

And when we were sitting around, a gang of us, we used to get comments, sometimes. Oh, you don't get black poofs. And then we did. A fellow came from the Central line. A black gay guy. And he was quite camp. Perhaps camper than anyone else.

camp fire   Those happy clappy carefree summer days   Buttercups and daises and little pan-

My first Pride was 1986, and that was with < > and < >. There were no floats at that point. Pride was still just people. There were banners but there was no organised… but I do remember < > spotting a couple of guys from Neasden, and waving to them. I mean this was when Pride was smaller. Yeah I know him, I know him, I know him… I've had him.

I mean I remember, you could go to Pride in mid 1990s and you could feel very alone, in this sea of people.

In 1991, we had tried… by this stage I was working in Travel Information… there had been an attempt to set up a London Transport Lesbian and Gay Workers Group so we met in London Lesbian and Gay Centre. But we never really managed to get the thing off the ground. I mean we did a couple of social events, I think we went ten pin bowling, but somehow we never managed to build up the momentum and really make this happen. We did have a banner, which I made.

Er, the banner had a pink and a black triangle one laid over the other which may have been an idea I had stolen from the Pride badge of 1986 or 1987, um, and TfL, or London Transport as it was then, were promoting travel cards with something called Supercar. It was actually a bus, but only the front third was a bus, the middle bit was a model, part of a Tube train, and then the back end of it was like a Network Southeast train. So kind of a drawing of that. It was on a sheet. I think either with paint or marker pens.

It's a pity… I destroyed it when I moved house.

Ladies and Gentlemen!
He kind of held up his forearm with a limp wrist, with the tunnel telephone box over the inside of his elbow, so carrying it like a handbag.

Most daymen and nightmen who shared stories had been at the Flower Market since they were teenagers, following relatives, either on the flower or fruit side. We talked about all the young men who had moved from Covent Garden, and later to Nine Elms, ending up in their sixties, teetotal, at the current site opposite the end of the new tunnels at Battersea.

He said: Oh no, no. The gays basically were there weekends and night times. We had the bar from the morning.

Well I used to stay behind and work behind the bar. And that was like... it was uneasy.

Nowadays it is more acceptable, and people just accept... which... I suppose it should be that way. But, you know, when you are an old dinosaur like me, you find it hard to... and each to his own, but when it is happening in a bar all around you, and... I'm old fashioned. But there was no shame to it... everywhere, in makeup and lipstick and high heels and suspenders.

Well, it was... they basically went through the night. I think he was an Irish guy. He had to leave Ireland, because in Ireland homosexuality was not accepted so he had to leave Ireland. And then he came over here.

Yeah, he never had anything to do with the morning Market. He would just like, he was a nice fella. He owned the place, basically, from lunchtime onwards, and then going into the evening when it was the gay scene. Very rarely see him in the mornings.

Saturday, because they had a gay night on the Friday, Saturday morning you had more chance of seeing these people.

Oh, just crazy gear. It was just guys with lipstick on, and makeup.

Yeah, they'd be from the night before, and I would think they would stay there. Yeah, but they used to black out the windows, and that's what they do in gay bars.

But, just round the corner, some of the pubs round here, even now, they are gay bars, and they are transvestite. I mean, you walk down there now and you wouldn't, you could see a lovely woman walking down the road and then it turns round and it's got a beard.

got in to the tarts And fairy cakes we had at tea together Together together

It was at the Tube station. I was coming up the ramp, and… all of a sudden she came into, I came into the Market, and he went up the pub, and when he turned round he had a full growth beard and I thought to myself... and it was… from behind, it was a model. A model. Tall, walking properly. And I'm not being funny. I mean, I'm a guy and I'm thinking, I can't believe that. I've just followed that bird up the road, and you know thinking what a lovely, shape and the way she is moving.

He was going up the Market Tavern, yeah. And I was going to work, yeah. I used to come on the Tube then.

No, always half eleven. Always eleven, twelve o'clock. It's earlier now. I started today at ten o'clock on a Sunday.

When he comes in at half one it is done. He wants to come in and get his orders all done.

I mean, last week, Valentine's, he had me in here every night.

I mean I don't really understand all that stuff, but this area, this whole area was known for it.

Yeah the Royal Vauxhall Tavern, yeah. That's still there. I mean, I go home that way. And you go there, and you stop at the lights and sometimes you don't want the lights to go green, because it is just amazing colour and they're holding hands and cuddling each other. Not being a voyeur and watching it… but it's another world going on here and you just think, like... whereas before it was hidden.

Yeah, yeah, that's why they blacked out windows in the Market. That was ideal there. They couldn't be seen from the street because it was up high. And the only people that went in there was the people that was in that scene.

At the Market Tavern, the charity stuff that they done was unbelievable. The barrow race. It was the fruit side versus the porters, and I was on the pitching in gang then. And we tried to get one up and they wouldn't let us do it. No, because you are not a registered porter. They raised it, seventeen thousand, for St Thomas in Great Ormond Street. For little baby incubators. And it was concocted in the Market Tavern.

When you tell people, they think oh, come on. Even my wife now… I used to tell her… she used to go, you ain't half a drama queen. And I say, well I'm telling you it as it was. And I've got to tell you this, so funny as well, is I remember the potman, you know, going round picking up all the glasses, and he used to go around, and he used to drink off the tables. And the governor went, look, I'll buy you a drink. And later he is sat in the toilet. And he's drunk, and has fell asleep.

together   Around the old camp fire   Where the mushrooms used to grow   And me muscles

But he has fell asleep with his trousers round his ankles, asleep. He was like that. Well some of the porters went in, and they've got hold of a daffodil…

> He said: When 'Blockbuster' used to come on, 'Sweet'… It's strange. We didn't like it then, but now in the Market we all give a cheer when that comes on, don't we? Reminds you of those times.

Just before we parted, we talked about whether they should be described here as 'dyke about town', which would have been accurate at the time they visited the Market Tavern, or 'queer about town' which is their chosen portrayal now.

She said: I was living in what was Frestonia, not while it was the Republic, but while it was still squats. Early 1980s, I would have been twenty-one.

When I saw it, well I thought, well I'm a big Martina Navratilova fan, so I was very delighted that a club had been named after her. I think I only went twice or something. It wasn't my scene, Martina's. It was too gay women-y for me, I'm afraid.

Like the Ace of Clubs. Not quite as bad as Gateways. I don't know how to describe it… the difference between dykes and gay women.

Yes. Very a-political. Very a-sexual in a strange way. Very un-queer in the way we would think about it now. It just felt like people were very closeted in the rest of their lives… just not my scene.

I remember Vivacious, definitely.

In the mid '90s… I remember thinking ah ha, this is more my cup of tea.

It was dark, which I liked. It was more cruisy. A look which I preferred, which might have been jeans and a white t-shirt, and some leather, not a lot. And definitely more political types. Definitely.

used to show Around the old camp Ahh Ahhh, Ahh Ahhh You better beware, you bet-

> Ladies and Gentlemen!
> At the beginning of the rails and at the end, we have a minimum distance we need to have to let the welders weld the rails. And after that, if there is a problem on the weld, they can repair it. So they mark one of the rails and as soon as they get the two rails on top of the blocks, with a ruler, like a square ruler, they mark the other rail, taking into account the position of the first one.

We spoke of all the gay venues which had vanished even before the bus garage arrived. One pub became a Starbucks. The variety of nights at the Market Tavern had catered for a wide range of crowds.

He said: Tuesday night.

My night? It was called The Hyperactive Clinic. Yeah.

No, I wish I had. It was a great flyer.

About 1982, 1983. It was about that time. I did it with a girl. She ended up leaving, and I ended up running it. And I ended up leaving cos I wasn't very happy with the situation. It wasn't particularly a very successful night, so I dropped it in the end. I'm trying to remember how long I did it for? Six months? Seven months? Something like that?

A band called Formula 5. I used to play in the '80s, 'Love Ride'. I don't remember who the artist was. 'Double Oh-Oh' by George Clinton, I used to play. I used to play 'Save Your Love' by Angela and Renee or whoever they were called. Um, what else did I play? Then I used to play things like 'Sensoria' by Cabaret Voltaire, urm, Gwen Guthrie, 'Hopscotch'. Because she became famous with 'Nothing But The Rent', but she made this really brilliant album much before that track and it was remixed by Sly and Robbie.

Yeah, I used to play that whole record cos it used to give me a break, because it was a forty-minute album. And it mixed itself. Do you know it? It is a brilliant album. *Padlock*, the album is called *Padlock*, by Gwen Guthrie.

You see, I was still finding my niche at the time. I was very new to it. Remember I was doing mobile disco.

It wasn't as trendy as The Bell. The Market Tavern didn't have the same clout as The Bell did, because it was predominantly like a sleazy leather crowd which used to go there. But what was good about < > is that he was quite open

ter take care You better watch out if you've got long black You've got the love I

minded. He could have really made that a seven night a week sleaze bar, if he had wanted to.

The Market Tavern was a bit more organised. The Bell was a bit more anyone could be part of it. The Market Tavern was <   >, who was a nice guy. But Sunday was lunch at the Market Tavern. I went there a few times.

Yes, I ate it. It was Sunday lunch. It was very proper and there were tables you got waiting staff on a Sunday, yeah.

But even the leather men who used to go down to the Market Tavern were a bit nicer. I think.

I didn't feel intimidated, cos leather was never my kind of scene at all. And even when it was my scene, it was the straight scene I was intrigued by, more. Because it was like, oh my God straight people are weird!

I think <   > should feature. He was probably not much older than us at the time, was he?

He had a lovely nature as well. I mean I used to fancy him because he was so nice. He was attractive, wasn't he? I mean he was a bit of a clone. But he was a nice clone.

The Readers Wifes began DJ-ing at a club night along the road. And then they began organising Friday nights at the Market Tavern. In common with many of those who worked or partied there, they vividly remembered the gay owner at the time, <   >, each for their own reasons.

He said: That's right. And, em, he would sort of… he didn't have… but he would put on his Irish records at the end of the night. And I don't know if it was to piss people off or to get people out. But he would come over and be kind of Alright boys! B..oy..s. Always drunk. Everyone was always drunk. Including ourselves.

> He said: Oh yes, I remember <   >. I didn't go to the funeral. I liked <   > very much.

He was quite… *very* Irish. He was quite intimidating when you first met him. He was the sort of person who you could kind of imagine you could offend or upset quite easily. And perhaps we did. And perhaps that is why I have that nagging sense in my head.

> He said: He was very, very nice to us. And he loved the music we played. And he gave me his Human League *Greatest Hits*. I remember that.

want   Come on and give   Oh, Danny boy, the pipes,   I only knew you for a while   I

> I've still got that, on CD.

He said: I think that is really sad, that once <   > went, there wasn't really anybody to look after it. He was the soul of the place, really.

> He said: The Pink. Yeah I was going to say. It must be The Pink. He must be in The Pink, cos the Market Tavern was a famous venue.
>
> Yes, the early 1990s is the worst time. Because it is just before everything starts getting digitised, but it's not far enough away for people to have archived it yet... for people to have loved it enough.

We first met a couple of years previously. She had been a promoter and performer for decades and we reminisced.

She said: Yeah, I remember the steps. I remember staggering down the steps at the end of the night.

And it had that nice balcony outside. You could go out there for a breather. Because you didn't have to go out to smoke, because of course you could smoke to your heart's content.

Big square balcony. There was two sets of steps. You went up one lot, and then round a corner, and up the last lot, and there were thirty-nine in all. And that's why <   > bought it.

Yes, that was true. And I know this because I used to work there, and he ran a quiz at Christmas at his Christmas party. And the person who won this quiz would get two weeks' free holiday at his villa in the Algarve. So of course we all did our best. And one of the questions was how many steps are there up to the door of the Market Tavern? And I've got a very funny habit of counting. I just count things. I just like counting. And so I would count, when I went up to work. And so I knew there were thirty-nine steps and he was absolutely flabbergasted that anyone knew the answer to how many steps there were. And then he said yes that's why I bought it. He saw it as very auspicious.

She read from a newspaper cutting: 'Door money and ten percent of the bar to Body Positive. Free buffet, and a present from Santa.'

It was a double door. It was matt black, painted matt black. Had a glass window. Opened outwards. And then you went into the vestibule. And on the right hand side... so that is where we used to sit, security. We both had stools, because you were allowed to sit down in those days. You weren't made to stand all the time. We could just sit on our little velvet covered cushion, and behind us was the

never saw your smile 'Til it was time to go   Time to go away (time to go away)   Sometimes

cloakroom. And we stood on the door and we just took the money, there and then. There was no till. People just gave us their two quid, and in they went.

Security, 1990 to 1993, on a Sunday. On a Sunday. Only on a Sunday. In fact, I did Saturdays as well. And that's how I knew that Saturdays were really dead, and that's how I got to run a Saturday night there.

So I worked on the door, which was a lovely job, except whenever there was any trouble, which was incredibly rare. But you know, you would get the occasional drunk and belligerent man, who just wanted to cause a fight. And I remember this happened on more than one occasion and someone would be kicking off in the back bar and the boys would go you go you go you go. He won't hit you. And I'd say but I don't want to go. You go. So I would have to go and kind of like, talk them down, you know, escort them off the premises. So that was always fun. And then I started working on Saturdays as well and they already knew me.

<   > was always giving money to charity. He was such a generous, lovely, lovely man, <   >. Honestly, he was really beautiful. A genuine person.

He didn't like people calling me <   >. He was like we are not calling you that. Ha ha ha. Because obviously then it was a really derogatory term. And so when I introduced myself he said what's your… lovely lovely Irish accent… which I won't do, as it would be insulting to Irish people… but he was like no no no we can't call you that. So what's your real name? So of course everyone called me <   >. Which was quite unusual for me. But, yeah. I thought that was quite sweet of him.

Ladies and Gentlemen!
To gain entry, you went up these concrete steps
which went up and then took it up, up, straight, and
then to the right and a little left up to the doorway.
With a great big neon sign which said Market Tavern.

At the Flower Market we sat in small offices which were surrounded by the upright displays made possible by Dutch buckets, the containers that have mostly replaced the long boxes which porters used to balance on their heads.

He said: Then I worked in the rose and carnation department. Used to have rose, carnation, freesias. And then you would have a spring department, you would have daffodils, the tulips. But we used to sell loads of freesia. Loads of iris. Loads of roses from Guernsey. We used to have loads of flowers from Guernsey. We'd have two hundred boxes of freesia in a day. And we could have five hundred boxes of roses coming in a day.

Guernsey was good for banking, and so their sons and daughters were going into banking and the flower trade went down. But then again we went up in quality.

Don't sell carnations now.

Oh probably fifteen years ago.

Just old fashioned. Old fashioned flowers that we sold were spray carnations, carnations. You'd have red, white, pink. You'd have light pink, dark pink. You'd have orange. You'd have dark orange. You'd have like cerise. And you would have all flecky, stripy ones. Carnations used to come in thirty sixes in a box, so when people say we sold, um, used to sell seven hundred boxes of carnations a day, that was all displayed.

We used to sell pallets of spray carnations. And Dutch flowers were five percent of our business, then, '90s. Now they are probably eighty-five, ninety percent of my business.

Now, hydrangeas in their season, are probably one of the most popular flowers now. With peonies, ranunculus. The quality is so much better today. We sell two hundred different flowers, compared to five or six which we concentrated on selling.

Would have gone when we finished work, probably around eleven am, when it re-opened. I never went when the porters used to go in there at five o'clock cos obviously I was working. But I may have gone up there to get my old governor out of there, <   >.

stay   Too late to stay   We'll always be together   However far it seems (love never

I worked for him when I was eight, yeah. He took me under his wing and he was like a dad to me really. And eventually I turned from tea boy, sweeping up, empty boxes, packing orders, and then ended up being a salesman. All through him, really.

They used to call him Charlie the Rose. And he always wore a rose. He used to sell roses. He was at the pub quite a lot.

He would have been in the Market Tavern for a swift couple of Scotches. But I would have gone and get him out a couple of times. Um, <   >, you are wanted in the Market. And then we used to stay in there until three o'clock when it shut.

Also, you would still even have the porters, some of them might have gone all the way through. And they would have been in a right state.

But the porters was right brothers, weren't they? You'd be drinking with you one day, and then you go into work, and they were all out on strike.

On the wall in the café at the Flower Market there is an old colour photo, taken by Clive Boursnell, of a flamboyantly dressed buyer with a large, elegant dog. Although no-one remembered the buyer's name, everyone knew the image.

He said: It's funny. As a business we have gay community built in. So when we see a gay… we are the most tolerant of working class… all that poofter this, that and the other, that's never been us. Because that's been the person who has come and bought the flowers off of us. I'm pleased that they can be out a bit more, and a bit more comfortable. And some of my nicest customers, and friends as customers are that way inclined.

Those who had been based at Parsons Green estimated that twenty percent of the drivers were openly gay there. We recalled the public information films when the crisis first took hold, and the struggles of gay and bisexual men, in those times.

He said: There was a lot of… I mean I remember the advent of HIV hitting the gay depots, and I remember the first guy to die from it.

As soon as a gay man went off sick, automatically round that depot… because I remember when a guy called <   > went off sick. And all round the depot, they were like… he's got AIDS. He's a gay man. He's got AIDS. And I said, no.

ends)   We'll always be together   Together in electric dreams   Because the friendship that

And there were some drivers would turn up with rubber gloves to take gay drivers off, and guards off.

Yeah.

The Company was like, *what*?

I was actually brought on to the Northern line for the opening of Edgware depot.

I applied for a job in 1983. And then told them I was going to start in 1984, so I started on 1 January 1984, as a station guard. And sort of thirty-five years later I'm still here. I've been here at Golders ten, eleven years now.

Train Manager.

We spoke of DJ-ing at The Bell and The Market Tavern, and friends and lovers no longer here.

He said: He just had a cold, and then died the next day. I mean all my favourite people I lost in that time. <   >,<   >,<   >,<   >.

She said: Dropping like flies from having a cold.

He said: We were like ambulance chasers, going from one hospital to the other. Funeral after funeral after funeral.

you gave   Has taught me to be brave   No matter where I go   I'll never find a better prize

Ladies and Gentlemen!
The gay guards at Parsons Green,
they were in a league of their own.

On the Historic Trackwalk, at the Battersea crossover box, we remembered all those London Underground staff who died from HIV and AIDS, scattering red ribbons amongst the concrete dust.

(find a better prize) Though you're miles and miles away I see you every day I don't have

Ladies and Gentlemen!
At the moment we are using one excavator to be able to install the blocks. And a forklift as well, to be able to move the material we are using to be able to build the track.

We met by the Train Manager's desk, on which sits a telephone.

He said: I answer and I say hello? Golders Queens?

Yes, I do. I *do*!

At that time, organisations such as London Lesbian and Gay Switchboard and Lesbian Line provided advice over the telephone: where to go on the scene, how to cope with coming out.

She said: It was an amazing woman who answered my call. It was in a phone box. I was thrown out on the street by my mum. I was living on my dad's floor in Sydenham, went to the phone box on the estate, and um, just said, I don't know what to do, I'm a lesbian. And this woman said, you know what, I'm not meant to do this but I'm going to meet you, and take you to a lesbian bar. And she did. And she met me, and she took me to a lesbian bar. And then my life took off. And I have recently put on Facebook I need to find this woman, who saved my life. Anyway, she took me to a lesbian bar which was amazing, because this woman called Jackie Forster was DJ-ing. Jackie Forster used to be like a radio star in the 1940s but she became a lesbian… she was in that film, *The Battle of Britain*, or something, as an extra. But she was an amazing person, an amazing woman who ran *Sappho* magazine. And was really upper class. But she ran this lesbian disco.

Warren Street, it was Warren Street. And it was a once a month disco, upstairs, in this straight pub. Where these women had this once a month disco run by a kind of grey haired… Jackie Foster.

No, this was like 1980.

It was 1983 when I first went into The Bell.

And then 1985 when we worked at the Market Tavern.

The Bell made the community which was able to do the Market Tavern.

The difference between The Bell and the Market Tavern is that The Bell was family, and the Market Tavern was the offshoot when the family just wanted some time away. It wasn't as public facing in that way.

This is the thing about The Bell, it was the only, mixed, gender mixed, club. So you would have a different mentality. Um, because you would have the leather men's clubs. You would never have a woman DJ-ing in a men's club. You would never have a gay man DJ-ing in a women's club.

They were the provincial queens who were in charge of the Bell. They should never have been put there. It was only the fact that we DJ-ed and the people who came there, that kept it going. Not because... it was in spite of them. We were constantly battling with them. They used to put big notices that... I used to be door staff on certain nights... we had to display notices saying only a certain number of females allowed in, you know, and clearly... they wouldn't empty the sani bins, they wouldn't put toilet roll in the women's toilets. On my nights I'd actually buy the toilet roll. They were vile, absolutely vile misogynists. They were so hated.

It was actually nice to have somewhere like the Market Tavern where there were no questions, didn't have to lick anyone's arse. You can have it as Chain Reaction, once a month. And it was so unusual for a women's night, on a Saturday.

That was so nice about <   >, right. Because although it was a sleaze bar in theory, he never had that misogynist, you know... He was such a nice man.

It was obviously a sleaze bar. It was all painted black and there were alcoves and there was a sort of back room thing. But it depended on what night you were on. If you came in during, um, if you walked in, say on a Chain Reaction night, it would be decorated with like sort of lots of camouflage netting, and drapes on the alcoves.

And so what we did as a collective, we would actually decide a couple of weeks before what the theme would be, and we would put on a show. There would be like the fashion show, for instance. Lots of people who designed rubber and leather gear to actually sponsor it and got catwalk in, got a motorbike in there. Had to empty it of petrol, of course. So a lot of work went into these shows, you know and they were absolutely fabulous.

Oh, well, a group of us. We would meet, you know, she had her parent's flat most of the time.

Yes, it was really posh. We would all kind of congregate there and work on what the next cabaret would be, what the next theme would be. Who was going to wear what, who was going to do what. You know, and just have rehearsals and meetings.

Yeah, six to ten of us. You know. Come up with a theme and act it out.

Well, there was a stage, wasn't there. And you could make a catwalk out of the bits of stage that were there. As you come in the door, it was, like, here.

You could kind of... with blocks of things around. It was all DIY. And it was, it looked good, in the end.

It was two years. '85 to '87. We even got mugs!

We were all on the dole. We all got grants, you know. We were squatting. This is the thing... we were kind of living slightly outside of the law and society. With our own societies, our own communities. And with coming of Section 28 which made us more, stronger, you know. Closing ranks with AIDS.

With the Market Tavern it was a place where we, as lesbians, were accepted to be ourselves and to express our version of our lesbian sexuality, in a safe space. Even though we were picketed and attacked by other lesbians.

I've been on the door of the Market Tavern and The Bell. What we used to do... we were there to make sure it was kept gay. And we weren't fascist about it, but we made sure that whoever came in was gay.

The most important thing was that we didn't rely on bringing in outside door staff. It was us who decided who came in and who didn't. We knew who were gay, and who weren't, you know.

You *know*.

We did used to ask those sorts of questions. Well, we did. We'd say, well, you know, name the gay clubs. What publications did you read? Some, um, you know, door staff would ask them to kiss each other, which I don't think was a good idea. But you know at least it was like the door staff you were meeting were gay. When now you come into a club and they are straight blokes from a security company. We were just there to keep the straights out. They don't know the difference between straight and gay people now. So they will let dangerous people in, as long as they look sober.

I must let you know that I DJ-ed at the Market Tavern just as myself.

It was live, you know. We didn't programme anything. It was just like what do we want, slam it on, and take it off quickly if it didn't work. If you lose the dancefloor. Fling the record behind you.

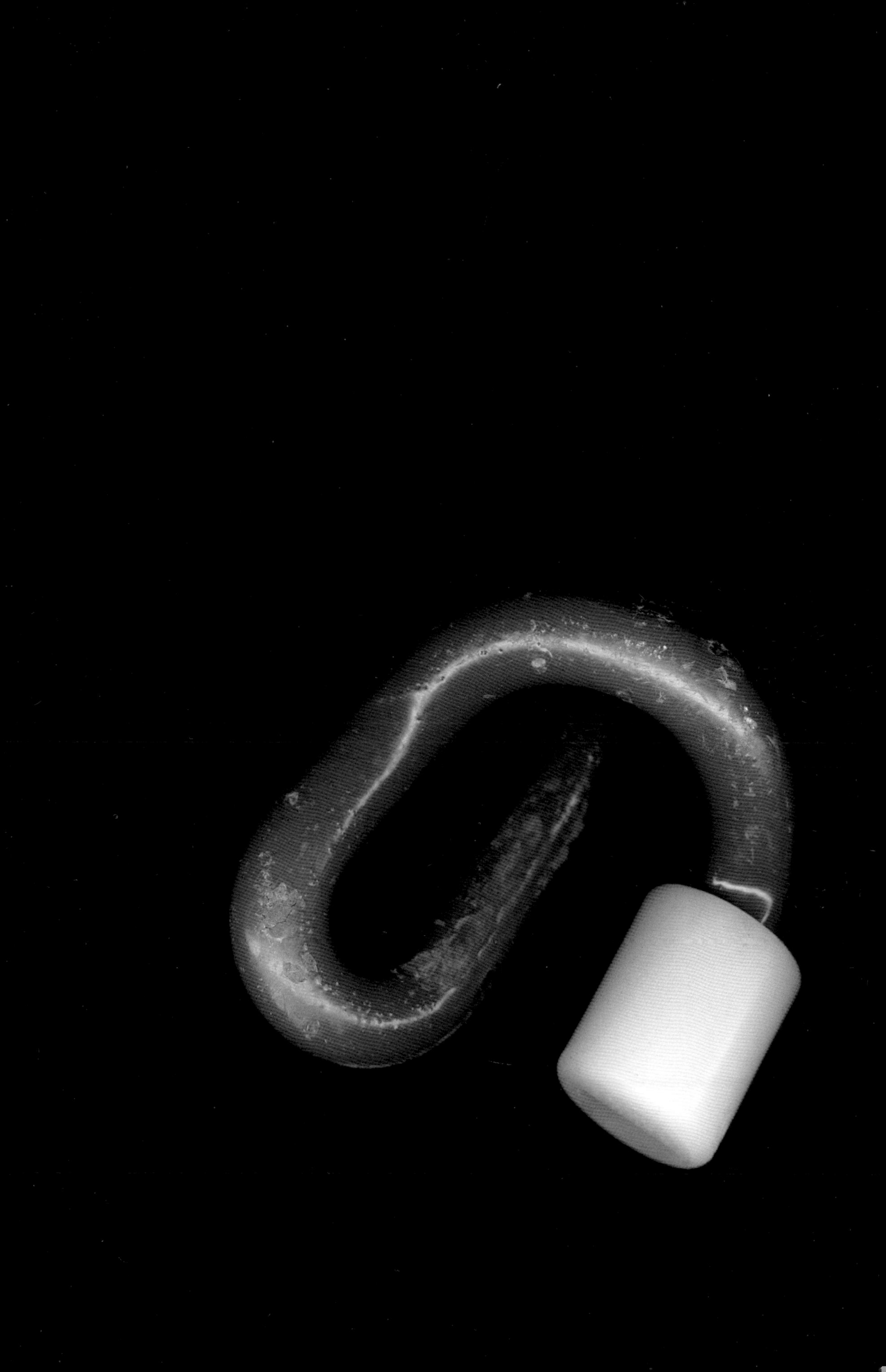

AINTED LOVE - GLORIA JONE

INTED LOVE - COIL

INTED LOVE - SOFT CELL.

AINTED LOVE - TONE LOC.

AINTED LOVE - ~~[illegible]~~ JAMES LAST.

EET SOUL MUSIC - ARTHUR CONLEY.

ERE'S A GHOST IN MY HOUSE - R. DEAN TAYL

EEDLE IN A HAYSTACK - VELVELETTES.

12	THE SNAKE	AL WIL
13	WEAKSPOT	EVELY
14	FOOTSIE	WIGAN
15	A LITTLE PIECE OF LEATHER	DONIE

READERS WIFES PLAY AT WIG'N'CAS ON ALTERNATE FRIDAYS AT

WIG 'N' CASINO

PHOTO BY CHRIS JEPSON

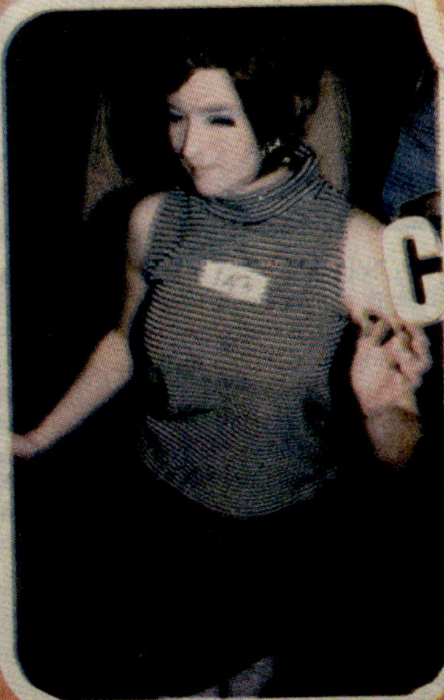

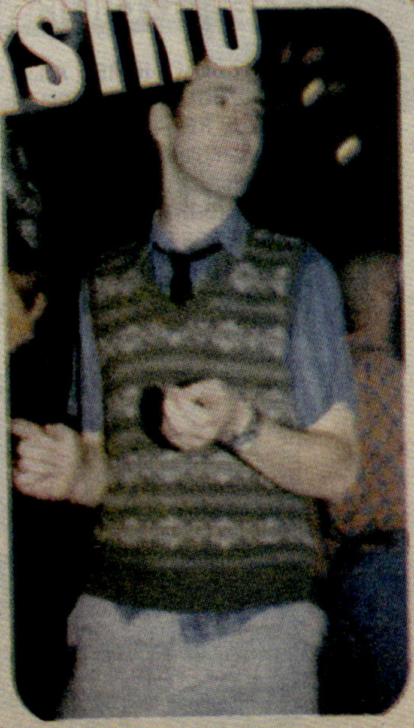

THE MOD SQUAD ARE BACK AND HAVE TAKEN OVER THE MARKET TAVERN WITH WIG'N'CASINO. THE READERS WIFES SPIN NORTHERN SOUL WHILE THE ONE AND ONLY AMY LAME HOSTS HER OWN GAME SHOW "READY, STEADY, GO." THE GRAND PRIZE LAST FRIDAY WAS A BRUCE FORSYTH ALBUM. I KNOW YOU'RE KICKING YOURSELF FOR MISSING IT, BUT AMY PROMISES ANOTHER TOP PRIZE FOR THE NEXT WIG'N'CASINO ON OCTOBER 4TH.

ALL PHOTOS BY ACM

Organ music on arrival and leaving St Peters
Performed by
Lee Walton
of the Market Tavern

Opening & prayer
by
Reverend **Ken Woolhouse**

Welcome from
Paul Wild

Music
"ALWAYS ON MY MIND"
Performed by
Susan Black

Maybe I didn't treat you
Quite as good as I should
Maybe I didn't love you
Quite as often as I could
Little things I should have said and done
I never took the time
You were always on my mind
You were always on my mind
Tell me
Tell me that your sweet love hasn't died
Give me, one more chance to keep you satisfied
....
Repeat

Reading
by
Mike McCann

Music
"STEAL AWAY"
Performed by
The Brixtonian Voices

I'm just going to put my hand up now and say my worst DJ-ing job at the Market Tavern was at KISS. It was after I stopped DJ-ing at The Bell. And it was when acid, well, no not acid even... it was when rave crept in.

No, '90s. It was '90s, yeah. This was like in 1995 or something and she asked me to DJ there, and this was when, you know, rave and everything had kicked in. When it was just like seamless beats, beats, beats, beats. We did stuff where each song had an identity, and people recognised it, and like love it, ah. So I tried to DJ at her thing, and it failed miserably. And it didn't work. I couldn't do it. And it was awful.

Ah, I don't know. I had this wonderful, you know, 'Hold That Sucker Down' by the O.T. Quartet. But I couldn't mix it with, any... I had bought all these rave compilations and didn't know what they were. And tried to kind of mix it in, and it didn't work. And my heart wasn't in it.

It was called KISS. It was a women-only... it was great. It was a great night at the Market Tavern.

I can't remember. But I failed terribly as a DJ, and it didn't work for me, because I was used to playing records that I knew the name of, and everything, not just tracks with the BPMs, you know. I couldn't do it. It just didn't work for me.

It was. It was. It killed it stone dead for me. The stuff that I was playing was just taken over by BPMs. It was killed by rave music and people off their faces on E.

Can I ask you something?

So when did you come out?

Ladies and Gentlemen!
At the moment we are using just a trolley
to move the small things through the tunnel.

Wig 'n' Casino took place every other week at the Market Tavern, alternating with Viva Apathy. We discussed the playlists. Viva Apathy starred The Divine David, who pioneered alternative drag. David startled audiences accustomed to the local stars of the time, including Adrella, who performed elsewhere.

He said: We were all in very much the spirit of the times. Anything is possible. Yeah, we will just do a Northern Soul night. It will be fine.

I think we probably said we need two record decks, two CD decks and twenty cans of Fosters, or something. And then we would just turn up and get ready.

Playing Soul records… those Soul records are like two minutes long. So you are talking about twenty-five to thirty songs an hour, and we were open for like five hours. Um, I was more tired after doing that club than any other, because we didn't, you couldn't put a record on and say phew. Everything was just bang, bang, bang, bang, bang. And we just didn't… cos the minute you cued up the song you had to be aware of what was next, and the one after that, and where you were going, so it was a very steep learning curve.

Nope, not really. We weren't experienced DJs… we were very passionate about, but we were not the right generation to have experienced it in the 1970s. And we were in the 1990s discovering a subculture from the 1970s, discovering… so it becomes quite meta, I think the word is, like a Russian doll.

And the vibe was like that. I loved it. We didn't have to try, the minute people walked in they would start dancing, before they had taken their coats off. It was great.

We weren't as reverential. A lot of Northern Soul collectors are very serious men… very serious, straight men. With their collections. Good luck to them cos they've introduced us to lots of great music. We were a lot more irreverent about it, even calling it Wig 'n' Casino, you know, is a sort of flippant way of treating a bit of cultural history.

Well, you can't really mix that stuff, because the beats wouldn't match, for a Northern Soul… not if you are talking 1960s Soul. They kind of fade out really fast, you don't get any… this is what I mean, you are constantly, like, 'It's fading out! We've got nothing next!' But I guess what we preferred, we did go for some of the more heavy Soul stuff, but we went for a lot of girl singers, so, you know, that was our, kind of take on it. We preferred the slightly lighter, slightly more

tell you now But let me tell you now But let me tell you now You've gotta hold that

tragic, emotional stuff, from the female side of Soul singers, than we did some of the more funky macho men stuff. So that's what we generally just preferred the sound of. So the club had a sound which was probably a bit faster.

From my Auntie Janet. My Auntie Janet was a South Londoner. She was very very cool. She still is very cool. She'd, um, been a big Soul fan in the 1960s when she was a teenager. And had ended up DJ-ing in some of the roughest pubs in the Old Kent Road. A woman, on her own, DJ-ing Old Kent Road, Walworth Road.

Just from going to the pub, I think. And like knowing, knowing the governors. And she would sort of like, saying I'd do it. I've got all the records. She worked for a record company.

> He said: I think there was probably a little bit of… I think I remember a little bit of resistance people who went to the Market Tavern because it was the Market Tavern. And it's like ufffh, that's Divine David, that's rubbish drag. It's not funny, or it's not this, or… his music is like, *old.* And I remember a few people saying, haven't you got anything more modern? Or can't you play… and that was when you felt like we were the new wave and these people were dinosaurs and we were like… and again… we probably got a bit full of our ourselves because the nights were successful and popular. So it does go to your head a bit. You do feel a wee bit trailblazy, or whatever that thing is.
>
> <   >is very good at looking at a crowd and telling when people had had enough of sort of, crowd-please-y or fast, and we'd just take it down a notch, and do techy sort of stuff. And when we were working with the Divine David, he would usually ask for, like Dawn Penn records, that he would be speaking over.
>
> There was a few things Divine David used to do, and he would kind of like speak to us and say… I'd like you to do this… I'd like you to play this same piece of record every, every time I do this. You know, so you would be kind of riffing off him. Or even suggest… he would say I'm going to come onstage in a cardboard box, and I've got a kitchen knife to cut myself out of it. Any music that you could think would be good for this? And I suggested 'My Coo Ca Choo' by Alvin Stardust, which is just the last thing you would ever think. So he did this thing with a kind of electric kitchen knife coming out of a box. Which was just… so you would understand why people, just expecting a sexy night out at the Market Tavern would be a little bit fed up.

He said: The Wig 'n' Casino wasn't a sleazy club. It was just *that* music and sleaze don't really go together. We have done sleazy clubs. But that music, um… however, but we did know what went on at the Market Tavern, the other gay nights, and I just loved that as well, the fact that, you know, it would be a

sucker down   You can lift your man up   Give him   No no no You don't love me   And I

completely… and also the fact that, the opening hours it had. I just… it was the same up in Scotland. My husband, my then boyfriend, now husband, and my father, both from Edinburgh. And Leith pubs, where they used to, kind of used to have fishermen and all sorts of stuff. So their trade was very much like the Tavern's, which was opening these hours where you just can't imagine... but of course it was the end of their working day... brilliant!

If we talked on one of the open stands, others would stop by, curious. Often a group would assemble, interrupting each other as we spoke about the times when the Market Tavern was part of the Flower side's morning routine.

He said: There was only one saleswoman. She used to drink up there, in the bar. She liked her fellas. She was a tomboy, wasn't she? She had hands like a man. That put me off straight away… would make me look inferior.

> He said: She was always up there with <   >. They used to cash in, didn't they? 'Cos they worked together, and then it went beyond being working.

He said: Yeah, and then he left his wife for her.

> He said: I was always a good friend of hers actually. I mean she was one of the boys, wasn't she?
>
> No, she is older than me by a couple of years. She'll be sixty-five now.
>
> The porter who used to wear the gloves, what was his name?
>
> It's like a flower thing, yeah. He had to wear gloves, he would come out in rashes.
>
> There are certain flowers here that I can't touch.
>
> If you got it, you got it, it will come out in you.
>
> You know when you come in, can you smell flowers?
>
> We can't. See. I can't smell nothing. And yet when I first came, the doors used to open, and...

know now No no no You don't love me Yes I know now Coz you left me Baby And I

At the time of the piling for the new skyscrapers, named 1 Nine Elms, we all sat in a room at Riverlight. We spread out old photos, drank beer and cider, and talked of the club nights.

She said: Cos I remember going in and the large room was first. It was first, cos the DJ box was up there on the left. And the bar was on the right. There were pillars and they had those kind of bricks you could see through. It was all very very '80s. Yeah, very industrial '80s. And huge air conditioning vents made out of aluminium, I suppose. But they were a real feature. They just ran all across the roof in this massive circulate air conditioning tubes. And camouflage nets. Every wall had a camouflage net. A dark green camouflage net.

She said: We put the camouflage nets up for Chain Reaction.

She said: Ah. I don't remember that.

She said: Chain Reaction. I can't remember the exact date, but early '87. Leather dykes who were based in Finland, or something. And they came over with this idea, so, um, we just went along to the show. They were organising it. But after a while they had to go back. And we took over. And started with all our mad cabarets. Which weren't quite as heavy duty. We wanted more of a light hearted element to it.

She said: I went when there was a band called The Darlings playing. I went then. I remember that.

She said: I took photos of my diary. Here you go...

She read out: 'Thursday, 29th January, 1987, um, we set off to the Market Tavern... inside was decked out in chains and lots of coloured hankies, with flyers to say what was what... <   > was playing the Violent Femmes cover of "Children of the Revolution". Um... duh duh duh... OK. It soon filled up with a marvellous assortment of leather clad posers. It was a marvellous atmosphere. Everyone was on the same side, for once.'

She said: I've got pictures of maybe eighty to one hundred people in it. And then the back bar was probably two thirds of that.

got no place to go now   No no no   I'll do anything you   You can bump and grind   Have a

Ladies and Gentlemen!
It was just like what do we want, slam it on, and take
it off quickly if it didn't work. If you lose the dancefloor.
Fling the record behind you.

For years, a room at the Coburg Street building near Euston station was the operational centre of the Northern line. Controllers and signallers were there, day and night. We talked about the challenges of the line, as well as the gender politics of being in charge, as a woman, in that decade.

She said: The thing is that if you do a complicated set of reforms, you have to make sure you have a driver left at the end, to take the last train. You've got to keep track of what you have made up and what you haven't, so you know that if you have made 43 to 37, 37 to 54, 54 to 36, and 36 to 43, which is what you started with, you've to make sure you've still got a driver for that first one.

I remember when I had been a controller for maybe about a year or so, and I felt like I really got the whole of the line in my head. So I could do something over here, and I would know it was going to do that over there, and what the impact was going to be. And it was really good. Because it really felt like I knew what to do with the Northern line. How to make it behave a bit better.

One of my great grandfathers was actually working on digging the Northern line. My mum told me. My grandad was born in 1921.

I did three years at Coburg Street.

Now it's all done by computer at Highgate.

But when I qualified as a controller at Coburg I was the only woman controller there. Um, there had been one before me, so I wasn't the first.

At Coburg, it was more like people were difficult. I was reasonably included in kind of whatever went on, when there were drink ups, or whatever, I wasn't excluded. But I felt I had to be better than the guys.

I've always been fairly out. I'm bisexual and I've always been fairly out about that.

I had to, as a controller, I had to be able to tell people what to do and make it stick. And say, no, I am the controller. We are doing it this way. Because that is what I've decided and that is my job to make that decision.

And you need to work with the Duty Manager, because you are moving crews around. If <   > was on the desk at Golders, I knew we would be alright.

good time You can twist and shout Let it all hang out But you won't fool the children of

I think you could do about forty-two or forty-four moves at Golders Green.

Like, different place to place movements you could do with a train depending on the signalling.

I liked being a controller. I'd been a signaller. I just preferred being a controller.

Because I absolutely loved it. You never knew what was going to happen. And you would have to fly by the seat of your pants, and skate two seconds from disaster, sometimes. If the controller says run that train via Charing Cross, the signaller might go but you've a really big gap coming up on the city, and the controller might say I know but I want you to run it by Charing Cross anyway. Or they might say thanks for pointing that out, I'll keep it on City.

The controller is supposed to have a view of the whole line.

When it comes to service recovery, after an incident, when you have to put the service back together, the controller... like Golders Green where you can do so many different things, you can also do an awful lot of interventions and when I was a controller, it was sometimes a little bit tempting to do too much at Golders. So, you would end up turning too many trains and generally causing congestion in this area.

Ladies and Gentlemen!
Now it is installing the rails.

We spoke about the worries that meant some drivers came out only after ten years, or more, at their depot. And about the longest tunnels of the Northern line.

He said: On the Northern line I think Golders Green was safest of the three depots.

Oh he was there already, yeah. I remember one of my earliest memories of the Northern line was… because I wasn't based at Golders Green, I was at East Finchley… but obviously you would get off at Golders Green to have a like meal break or whatever. Then <   > had peroxide hair. I remember walking past the counter and it was like, oooh hel-lo.

I have a huge amount of time for him. But my earliest memory is when I was twenty, walking past him. So I think sometimes it takes just one person who is unashamed, and unapologetic for who they are, that it just becomes that beacon, almost. The fact that <   > was happy to be <   > meant that maybe other people were more comfortable being themselves at Golders Green.

So if you were on the Northern line it was the place to be, and probably thanks to <   >.

Back in the 1990s it was still not a particularly desirable job. So after World War Two it was pretty much the back of the queue in terms of recruiting staff. Which is one of the reasons why the Underground started having to look overseas. I think right up to the 1990s it was quite an undesirable job. They had to put up posters saying please come and work for us. Things have changed massively now.

Now we do directly recruit train drivers for Night Tube. An advert will go online and they will have tens of thousands of people applying, within like minutes. It has changed massively, because I think the whole employment market has changed. And I would say, probably testament to the strength of the unions, our pay and conditions have been protected. While there has been this attrition elsewhere, and zero hour contracts.

Yeah. This is the thing. I think people recognise more and more, OK, it is functional, um, but if you do want a hopefully secure job for the rest of your life that will pay the mortgage, then it is not a bad bet.

I was a direct recruit guard to the Northern line in 1997. So twenty-one years ago. I was a university drop out. I was working in night clubs. I was working on the gay scene at that time. Realised I probably needed to get a real job. I saw a poster

falling rain   I gotta rolls royce cause its good for my voice   But you won't fool the children at Old Street Tube saying seventeen grand a year, who wants to be a guard? And I thought, yeah, I could do that. I had always had an interest in trains and the Tube, anyway. It was actually on a short term contract and that is because at that point they were getting rid of the 1959 stock trains. And those were the last trains on the entire Underground that needed guards.

Twenty, I was twenty.

I enjoyed the practicality of working with the trains. So I could start to see quite rapidly that I could make a fist of a career with the Underground.

Much of the 1990s if you wanted to be a guard, the only line you could do that on was the Northern line.

You land at your depot and I was assigned to East Finchley. And I guess maybe then I wasn't very outgoing. I was quite shy. I was very young. And there is a real, you know, mess room culture. And banter. And you can't sit in that seat. That is such and such's seat. And it was quite an intimidating environment for someone my age.

It wasn't the most pleasant of environments. So I remember, from an LGBT perspective, I remember one day, there was an episode of Jerry Springer being played on the TV in the corner, and there was one of these I've got a secret to tell you darling. And this big burly guy comes in dressed as a woman. So it is a shock for the wife, and everything. And I remember one guy stood up on his chair and started hurling homophobic abuse at the TV. Like 'batty men!', and 'burn in hell!' and all this kind of stuff. And, so if I was already a bit nervous and shy, I was even more so.

I have no doubt, well I know for certain, that there are still a lot of unsavoury attitudes out there. It is just everything is more covert now. It was cool to stand on a chair, in the middle of the mess room and hurl homophobic abuse at the telly. You couldn't do that now. Well, I hope not, anyway. Well, certainly not on my watch here.

In 2011 I switched back to being a Train Operations Manager here.

Well that kind of sets the scene for the type of environment that as a relatively shy young gay man you didn't particularly feel welcome in, and didn't particularly want to stick around in. And the set up being a guard is you are paired up with a driver for the whole day, so you see them when you are changing ends at Edgware, hi, changing ends at Morden, hi, and then you spend the entire meal break… And then you really do start to get a grilling. Oh, have you got a girlfriend? Are you married? What does she do? And, you find yourself, unfortunately, being drawn into, because it is easier than telling the truth, you start to allude to stuff, even to the point of fabricating a bit of an untrue back story. You generally feel as if it is the safest thing to do. Because you would only be with that particular driver for that shift, and then the following shift it would be a different driver, so you might not get round to that driver for another couple of months.

I'm kind of ashamed of it now, but it was a self-preservation thing, I think.

And I had heard about this mysterious depot called Parsons Green, which was the pink depot, so I thought I'll put myself down for Parsons Green. Um, and early 1999, so I've only been on the Northern line for, uh, eighteen months, and I got my call to go to Parsons Green on the District line as a driver, had two and a half years driving there, and it very much was the pink depot. So that was a great experience as a driver, contrasting the Northern line. I'd put in the nomination to go to Parsons Green pretty much as soon as I passed out as a driver. I just felt, I had to, like, grin and bear it for a few months, and then, you know, I'd be moving.

About a year of guard, and then about six months of guard-motorman before I transferred to the District line.

It would be snide comments. So, you know, and this isn't a direct quote, but it would be something like, you know, have you got a girlfriend? If you haven't you better put your name down for Parsons Green, mate. You kind of find out immediately. It was part of the jungle drums, part of the folklore. You know, that if you are on *that* bus, put yourself down for Parsons Green.

I think sometimes it can just take one or two prominent people. So I think, um, there was quite a notorious trans driver at Parsons Green. Back in the 1970s. And all it takes is just one person. Oh, there's an openly transsexual driver at Parsons Green, therefore that's where all the Nancy boys go. But then it becomes a self-fulfilled prophesy.

Uh, no. Definitely not. Even by the time I got there, she had gone.

So, and other rumours, I think possibly untrue, like Julian Clary used to be a guard at Parsons Green. So, before you know it, it becomes part of folklore.

I think he was on the Underground. I mean, I've never met him to ask.

I think it is just one of these urban myths, um, that just gets baked into being fact.

So yes, if you are gay and getting on the Underground and not particularly loving life wherever you are, and you hear about this fabled depot where actually maybe you won't have to lie. And you would just fit in, then it kind of attracts people.

And it was absolutely what I hoped it would be.

So, even, all the straight drivers would say oh are you alright duck? Are you alright, darling? And not in a kind of disparaging way, but in a quite homo-friendly, like, no chip on their shoulder, way.

Yeah, so it felt very welcoming. You didn't feel like you needed to construct a tissue of lies. It would just be… I didn't have a partner then, but you wouldn't have had any compunction, saying right from day one, I've got a partner, he does this. Um, whereas you wouldn't have done that at any other depot, at that time.

On the old Northern line trains you were the leading single door on the last carriage. So you just had this metal bar that you'd place across the gangway, so customers couldn't… so they could still get to you, but it was a kind of visual thing, saying, this is the guard's bit. You'd put in this key, which is just like a big spanner, basically. And that was your kind of office, this small, couple of meter square bit of Tube carriage.

You are surrounded by the travelling public. You had a little fold down seat, one on each side. And you could, if you were minded to, engage with the customers, which I really enjoyed. So, you could just have a chat to them, because what else are you going to do between each station?

I guess there was always the element, you know, gaydar. So going through certain areas, it would be spot the gay punters on the way to wherever, Market Tavern, you know. So if you were minded to Friday or Saturday night… to be honest, I quite liked doing a late shift coming down the Charing Cross branch, because there would be people going out to wherever, Soho. Um, and I guess that would be the same anywhere, but being a guard you are immersed by the customers in the last car. So, you know you generally can… again I flirted with people, eye contact, whatever.

Checking for the signal, making a judgement call when to close the doors, and then you would remain with the doors, and this is like massively unsafe, now, but you would stand in the open doorway as the train pulled out of the platform, watching the platform. Obviously if there was someone who you had annoyed, who didn't get on your train, you'd often have a barrage of beer cans, or spit, or whatever. Obviously lots of swearing, as the train pulls out.

Some of the areas the Northern line goes through used to be a lot seedier, so your Tootings and your Balhams and places like that. I mean Clapham, there are all these places which have upped and come, now. Like twenty years ago, they were still quite scary, Angel, Old Street. Places which are kind of hipster and yuppified now.

Yeah, it was like the Bronx before. If you are alone late at night, and they are only other person in that carriage, and they decide they want to be your friend, or whatever, you have nowhere to run.

The overriding sense of the Northern line is tunnel. So you go into a tunnel at Morden, if you are going via Bank, it is seventeen and a half miles before you get to Finchley. It is a long way. It is a lot of tunnel. And I think one of the issues is, you get down to Morden… it is most painful on a lovely summer's day… you see a brief glimpse of sunlight when you change ends at Morden and then you go back into the tunnel again. Um, so leaving that behind, I didn't miss at all.

I guess there was something just very evocative about those old trains. Um, because they were about to be withdrawn, they were very tired. They were the bare aluminium bodies, so they could never clean the graffiti off them properly. So, the outsides of the trains had lots of ghosts of graffiti. They used to have lovely London Transport transfers on the side which had all been buffed off from trying to get the spray paint off. The interiors were all wooden. The predominant moquette was a kind of blue and green one. But then it is how you generally tell the trains that came off the Central.

It was incredibly dirty. So modern trains have electromagnetic brakes, mainly. So there is no actual friction, brake block on wheel to stop the train, it is essentially the motors going into reverse. So it applies the resistance to slow the train down. The old Northern line it was one hundred per cent friction brakes, so every single time a train stopped it was brake blocks rubbing on wheels. And brake dust.

It is a weird mix of resin and iron. So you were basically constantly breathing in this cocktail of resin and iron filings. And you were at the back of train, obviously. If the train had what was called sticky brakes, so they weren't releasing particularly well, as you were hanging off the back of the train, watching the platform, it would feel like someone was throwing sand into your face. You would actually have particles of brake blocks hitting you.

On the '59 stock.

Yes, although there were a few 1972 trains stocks knocking around. They look exactly the same but there were a few cast off 1962 stocks from the Central line but they basically looked and drove the same.

Yeah, so you were basically in this cocktail of brake dust all the time.

Even if you looked in the creases of your face, there would be brake dust.

People say now oh health and safety gone mad. And it's like, not being funny, twenty, thirty years ago, Zebrugge, Kings Cross fire.

Precisely. So it is the right thing to do.

The trains were just very noisy, in terms of the moan of the motors was a lot, like, louder than modern trains. The compressors that kept the air charged, they'd kick in and out. So it would just sound this massive loud churning whirring noise, on and off. And even the suspension of the trains was very crude. It was something called Metalastic, and it was layers of rubber and steel. And it used to make this really alarming creaking and banging sound. So as the train was swaying going over points it just sounded like someone hitting the bottom of the train with a hammer. So just general evocative noises, and the smell of the brake dust. And just general wooden interiors, fairly gloomy. It doesn't sound particularly nice, but if you could kind of bottle something, it would be nice just to experience that, again.

Just one final thing. Not that I had to have my mind made up. But when I went up for motors, when I had to do my driver's training, there was another... oh this guy might be worth speaking to, his name is <   >. He is now a Metropolitan driver. He was a guard at Golders Green, we were both in the same motor's class, training to become drivers, and he sniffed me out. Straight away. So, but of course he was telling the other guys in the class, so I started getting probing, knowing questions. And I was actually at Ashfield House at exactly same time as my flatmate. We both resolved to join the Underground at the same time. So when I was doing my training, he was doing his ticket office training, so we were both there at the same time. So who is that guy you keep on talking to? Is that your boyfriend? And I went no, no, no. So I was somewhat in denial to them. I was denying he was my boyfriend, cos he wasn't. And I guess it would have sounded like yeah, yeah, to everyone else.

And when I got back to East Finchley, someone had stuck up a notice on the wall saying these are the next ten people to come out at East Finchley. And it was basically outing ten of us.

Yeah. I don't think it was <   >. But I think it was one of the guys I was training with, cos a few of them were East Finchley guards... going back to become East Finchley guard-motormen.

There was just like, these are the next ten people to come out. Some were kind of joking, clearly straight, others were like, kind of.

I can't remember. But I was number one on the list.

If there was ever a reason for me to want to leave, that was like one of them.

The Market Tavern... I just remember that you had to go up, it was the bottom of a tower, which has obviously now gone. And you had to go upstairs to go to it. And I remember it was quite dingy. You would see famous... so Jean Paul Gautier used to like going there, so you would see him, Mark Almond, people like that. So, yeah. It was just one of many places to go.

Ladies and Gentlemen!
There were pillars and they had those kind of bricks
you could see through. It was all very very '80s.

After the shafts were dug at Battersea, FLO [Ferrovial Agroman Laing O'Rourke] started constructing the tunnels with sprayed concrete lining. But most of the new track sits in spaces formed using two, six metre diameter tunnel boring machines, one named Helen and the other, Amy. Both machines locked together concrete rings as they moved along, under the local roads (Nine Elms Lane, Post Office Way, Ponton Road, Wandsworth Road, Wilcox Road, Wilcox Close, South Lambeth Road, Old South Lambeth Road, Hayford Avenue, Meadow Road, Fentiman Road, Carroun Road, Cottingham Road, Trigon Road, Claylands Road, Elias Place, Hanover Gardens, Kennington Park Road, Harleyford Street, Camberwell New Road, Kennington Oval, Brixton Road, Bowling Green Street, Clayton Street, Kennington Green, Kennington Park Road, Aulton Road, Ravensdon Road). And to connect the new tunnels to the existing line, a larger tunnel was excavated around the ancient cast iron rings, which were then carefully extracted. On site we often talked about the satisfaction of the engineers with what had been accomplished.

She said: When I came here we were in the excavation of the shafts, and after that I was involved in the SCL [Sprayed Concrete Lining] tunnels. In the step plate junction as well. That's the connection as well, with the Northern line.

Then after that the TBM was dismantling to be able to take every piece of the TBM out through the shaft. And now I'm involved in the track as well. I think that step of the project is less interesting, talking about engineering. But it is quite interesting to know how it is working.

Drivers who joined London Transport before the 2000s had all been trained on at least two models of stock which were taken out of passenger service when Automatic Train Operation arrived. We chatted about the transition from guard to motorman, the term now replaced by driver-operator.

He said: Well, er when I moved from Scotland in 1987 I used to work in the city, and I was on my way home, in the autumn of '95, and got chatting to a train driver.

Um, I'd always been a bit fascinated by the railways. So we were chatting about it, and I asked how did he end up as a driver and he said, well you go in as a guard, and they are looking for guards on the Northern line. So just to get away from boring office politics in the City, with the intention of only doing that for six months, I decided to become a guard. And I got accepted, and they posted me to Golders Green. And after being here for six months, they started looking for drivers. Cos they were about to bring in the, er, '95 stock trains which we have now, because previously we had the older trains. But those new trains had been delayed, so they needed drivers to be trained up, so that is how I started.

So I came for six months and twenty-three years later I'm still here.

Never been anywhere else. Never done any other line other than the Northern line. And I've never been at any other depot apart from Golders Green.

I never hear people mention Parsons Green now. I used to, when I first started. Yeah, you used to hear that, yeah. Ooh, he's come from Parsons Green… Woaah-hu-heah!

Day one it was a bit like being in the army. Because… oh gosh, the first day you showed up in White City railway training centre and you went and you sort of had an induction day. And it was either later on that afternoon or the next day that you went down to Acton, and that is where you got your uniform.

And it really was like being in the Army. You went in and they went, size, trousers, hat, and all that. And you left with this great big bundle of clothes. And the next day, put it on. And that was you.

It was social, but not social for the right reasons. Cos you were, I mean, as the guard's role came to an end, the Northern line was the only one with guards, so there was a lot of people using the Underground every day who had never seen a guard, and then there was a thing where suddenly they turned up to make a journey on the Northern line and there was this guy standing there. Used to get them trying to force themselves into the guard's door and you kind of asked can you use another door? Conflict. Flashpoint. Oh don't tell me what to effing do. So as it became closer to the end I thought it became a lot less pleasant. And I suppose passenger numbers were increasing, the trains becoming unreliable so they were breaking down more. So it was becoming harder to be a member of staff in that front line environment.

She said: For me, it was the step plate junction, because at that moment we were working every day with drawings, and, the plan was changing depending on the movement, or some problems, or just things we had, unexpected, in the step plate junction.

He said: '59 stock, '72 stock as well. The two older stocks.

All about the track signals, stop and proceed.

Learning about compressors. Coupling up and uncoupling.

In 1995 this was very much male. Very straight male.

Yeah, he was here. But he wasn't sitting in the mess room.

And there were very few women. Very few women.

She said: Ah, that's the electrician... sparky. He is now getting the lights ready, the traffic lights we are using to be able to communicate between the pump and where everyone is working on the pour.

We are also using radios. But this is also another way, to make sure if we need to stop because of something, he is going to know straight away if we need to stop pumping to avoid any accident. Mmm…

[Loud crashing sound]

Ah no. It's OK.

He said: Well I'm very good at fitting in. Like, so I'll change to suit how I am. So you don't kind of stand out. He says. OK, I stand out. But that is nowadays. Weren't then.

It was all technical. It was about signal overlaps.

She said: Yes, exactly. It was quite interesting because, well everything was new for me, it was a lot of different things and the plans were changing. And it was quite, er, different for me to be working underneath the loop, and making the structure to be able to hold the loop, and make sure walls in place.

The tunnel. The tunnel of the Northern line.

He said: And if they were to suddenly say we are getting rid of ATO [Automatic Train Operation], and we are bringing back the red and green signals. And we've got some '59 stock trains that we are going to refurb and bring back, I would be well happy.

She said: It was still more than one hundred years ago. And to be able to do that extension. We were doing the connection in the step plate junction.

To do this we did excavations of that area around the tunnel where the train was running.

it all hang out But you won't fool the children of the revolution No you won't fool the chil-

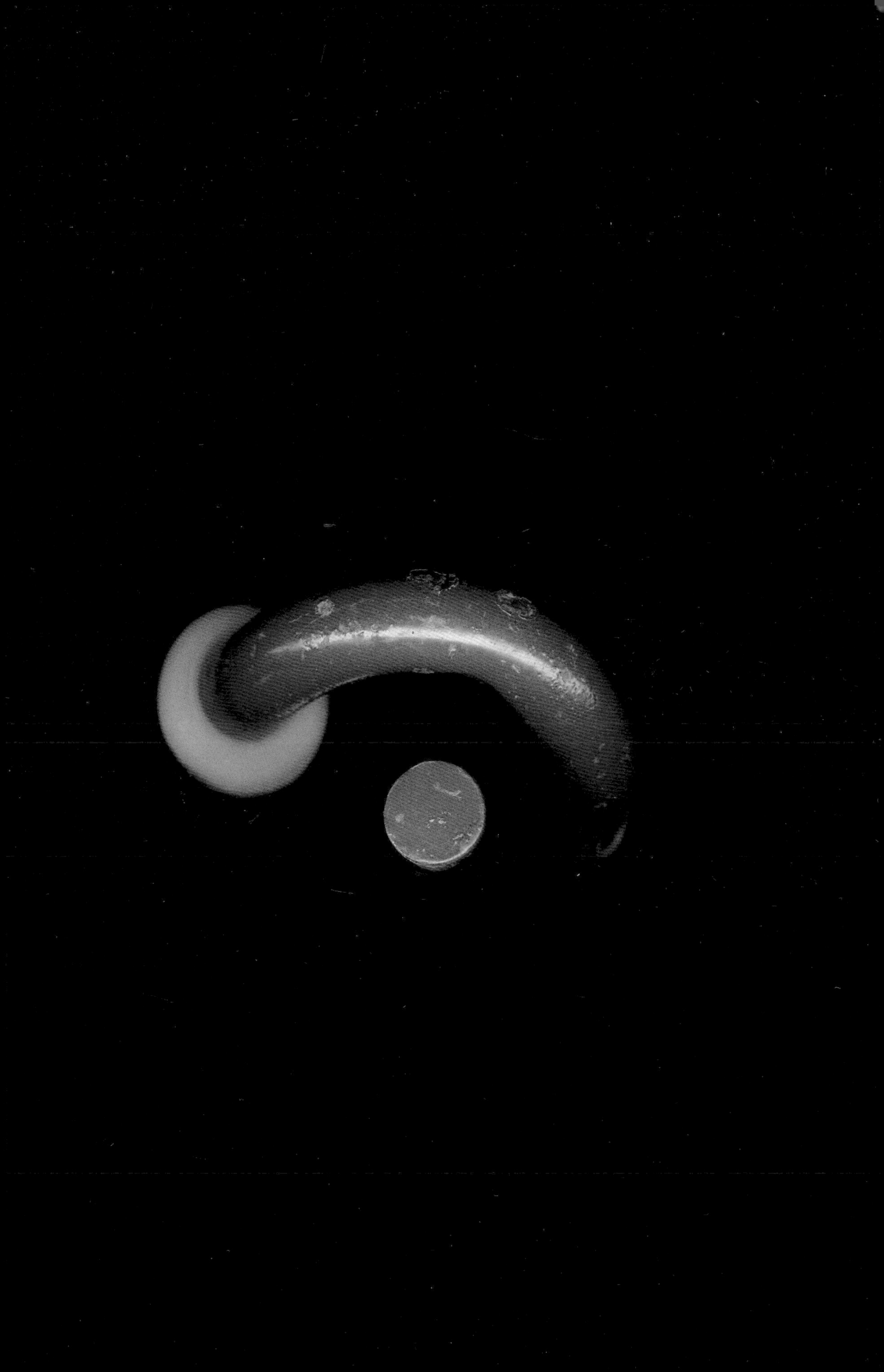

ARL'S COURT
WHO'S LOOKING AFTER YOUR NEST-EGG?
It's the next best thing to being there.

322
3563

3638

3612

PARSONS GREEN
0 5 7
District line

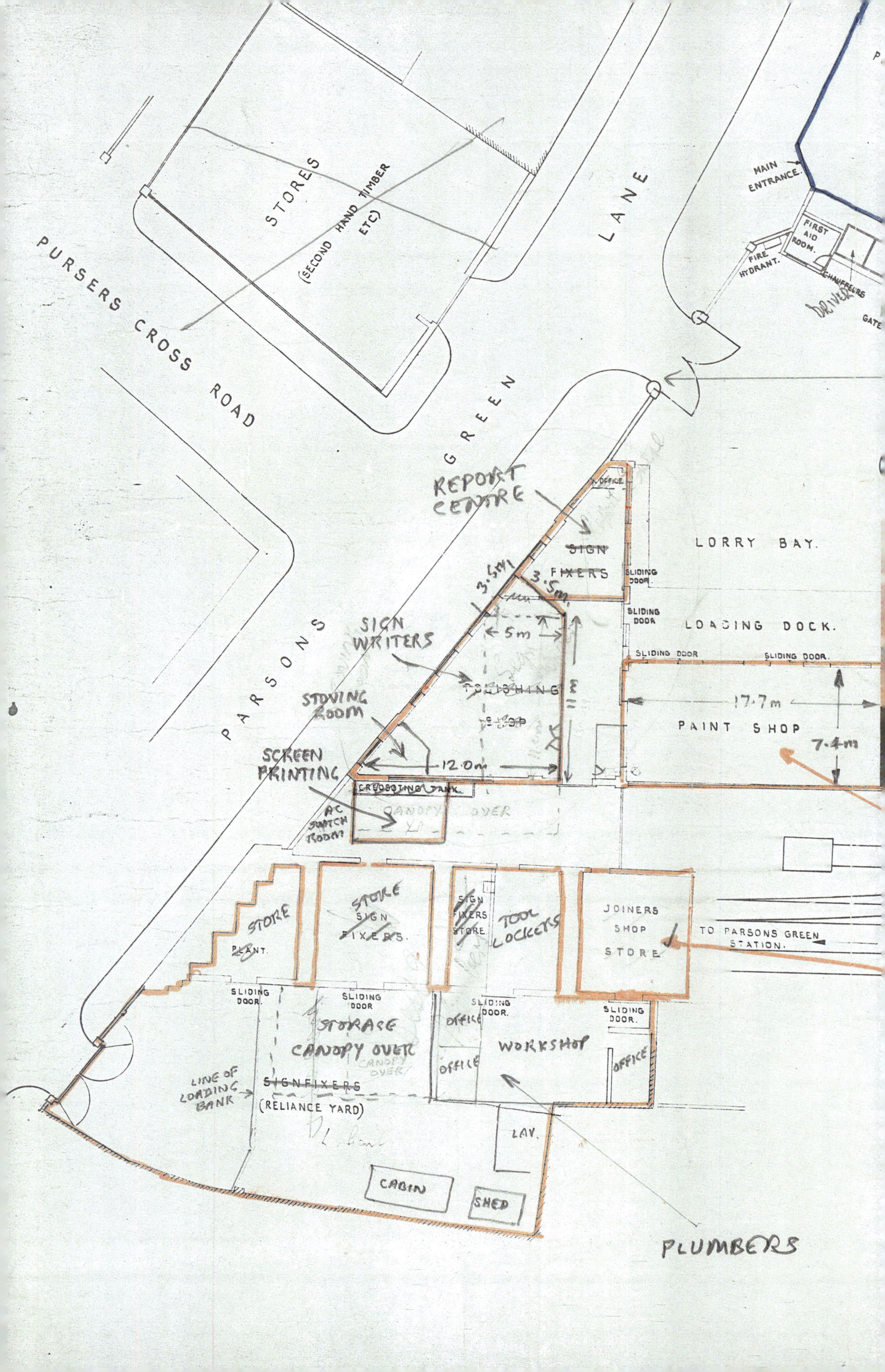

STORES
(SECOND HAND TIMBER ETC)
PURSERS CROSS ROAD
LANE
MAIN ENTRANCE.
FIRST AID ROOM.
FIRE HYDRANT.
CHAUFFEURS
GATE
PARSONS GREEN
REPORT CENTRE
OFFICE
SIGN FIXERS
LORRY BAY.
SLIDING DOOR
LOADING DOCK.
SIGN WRITERS
FINISHING SHOP
STOVING ROOM
SCREEN PRINTING
12.0m
5m
3.5m
SLIDING DOOR.
17.7m
PAINT SHOP
7.4m
CREOSOTING TANK.
CANOPY OVER
AC SWITCH ROOM
STORE
PLANT.
STORE
SIGN FIXERS.
SIGN FIXERS STORE.
TOOL LOCKERS
JOINERS SHOP STORE
TO PARSONS GREEN STATION.
SLIDING DOOR.
STORAGE
CANOPY OVER
WORKSHOP
OFFICE
LINE OF LOADING BANK
SIGNFIXERS
(RELIANCE YARD)
LAV.
CABIN
SHED
PLUMBERS

After that, we stopped the train for a couple of weekends. And also for a week, to be able to do the proper connection with the rails. And let the trains come through in the future.

He said: You can still drive them manually, if you want.

I do, sometimes. They don't like it in the rush hour, because they want everybody to keep up. But outside the rush hour, if you want to stick it in Protected Manual, they don't have a problem, as long as you keep up with the timetable. They don't have a problem with that.

Well the thing is that it was the ATO which put me down that road to part time. Cos I just thought I can't sit and do this. It is doing my nut in.

I was just thinking the old pictures you've probably seen of people digging the tunnels for the original Northern line. Because I think there is one, where there is something like twenty, thirty men, all you know, standing near the tunnelling thing. And it just would be interesting to think if, you know, the current statistic of one in eight, or whatever it is, that in that picture… there were men in that picture who were maybe struggling with something. Or, you know, perhaps they didn't struggle with it.

I mean, what was it like in 1890?

Well, I mean, there were bars, and it was a thing. Like people did know about it.

She said: We stopped it two weekends to be able to break all the old tunnel. And after that, last Christmas the train was stopped for a week, to be able to build the track in that area, and to be able to do the connection with the rails.

They are not going to need to stop it again.

He said: Now, are you talking about the Market Tavern, or the Vauxhall Tavern? There was two places at Vauxhall.

That's what you are on about? Oh, I thought you were on about the other one. Oh well, your question before I misunderstood. Oh I was in there a lot, yeah, yeah.

Ah. Well the nights I used to go to the Market Tavern, um, well they had all kinds of nights at the Market Tavern.

Basically, what it looked like, well, I always got the impression… it just seemed like a concrete box.

You had to go up some stairs, concrete, and went in.

She said: They are still working engineering hours, at night, to be able to fix a few things in that area, but it is not like before, where you need the whole day to be able to break the tunnel and after that leave everything clean and safe, to let the train going through.

He said: Well, it was a very mixed crowd. But I was more interested in the leathery, army, type, guys. That's… well, still am. But they don't really exist anymore.

That was probably the beginning of the partial decimation of the gay scene. And it's all splitting up and fragmenting. You know I have conversations with friends of mine who used to go to the Market Tavern years ago. And they feel there is less and less of a… a support network where you would pick on a pub, you know, let's say at the moment, probably my likely place is Comptons.

She said: I'm going to remember all the people I knew working here. I was working with Irish people. It was really good. They are really professional and they have a big experience in tunnelling.

Most of them have relatives working in tunnels and, well, I remember once I was working with three people from the same family. It's quite usual.

Ya, ya, quite usual to find relatives working here.

Erm, it was a brother, and also the uncle of one of the miners.

Hmmm, they were working in mining, and also they were working building the rings in the step plate junction, along the tunnel. And well, in that moment it was like a real mining works, because the space where we were working was really small.

Maybe sometimes we were working a metre and a half by a metre, high.

It was quite, erm, difficult sometimes to be working there, like, eight people.

I was thinking in that moment, I was lucky to have started working here and seen the whole process. If you start just at that point, and need to go into that small area, I'm sure it wouldn't work for me, because you feel like really…

Yeah, exactly, that's the word. That's the word. Yeah.

Claustrophobia, yeah. Yeah, yeah yeah.

good for my voice But you won't fool the children of the revolution No you won't fool the

He said: But even Comptons is becoming, can I use the word, diluted? In that it is not exclusively gay. Or it seems to be that they will let anybody in, really.

Like the Ritz after the War. They will let anybody in.

And, erm, yeah. So I feel that these places are disappearing. What is replacing it, I'm not really sure. People are connecting, probably apps. Which I completely don't get.

I don't get that at all.

I think it causes people to be extremely anti-social.

And neurotic.

And also it causes some people, maybe not everybody, to treat other people like a commodity rather than an actual person. They have a desire to have sex so they just flick through something a bit like the Sainsburys catalogue and you think I'll try that one. And there you are.

I think it is the heart of this thing, which I always regarded as Soho, or Earl's Court, or, years ago, the Vauxhall area. That's all changing. Earl's Court has completely gone. There is no gay place in Earl's Court at all. And there used to be four or five, six, places.

But that is the funny thing. You read in the paper now about LGBT this and it is all, how, you know, how, it is all people being picked on. And I'm thinking it can't be worse, now, surely, than it was in the 1980s.

She said: The step plate junction? Just shovels.

Yeah, no, so, diggers as well. To be able to break the, the clay. But before that, they were using an excavator, but that was before we started the step plate junction. And it was just to be able to excavate the… we were doing like a metre section, and in that moment they were using the excavator.

He said: I seem to remember inside as well, there wasn't any white lighting, it was all either red, green or purple. You know, and depending on what outfit you wore, looked bleeding awful. If you were wearing like green combats and a red light, it didn't look very good.

Yeah, I seem to remember that. There wasn't any light, you know, it was all artificial.

> You know, if the Black Cap was still open, I'd probably be in it almost every single night.

She said: So it was a movie I enjoyed a lot when I was a kid. And probably I never think about me, in the future, a woman working in a tunnel, and going to work like with a gang around seven men, you know! And people singing that song.

The protagonist is *Blancanieves*

Blancanieves? And the seven small…

Seven dwarfs? And?

Snow White. Snow White, exactly.

Because that song is… I can't sing it now, but there is, it is talking about mining. You know which song I'm telling you…

Exactly. Yes, some people… not this gang. But some people I was with in the SCL tunnel, some of them. Well, all together, you know. Because when we realised that it was the situation, more or less.

Sometimes we went down into the tunnel, just singing the song. It just have English…

Yeah, but because of the sound, I recognise and I realise it, more or less.

shout Knock yourself out But you won't fool Heigh-ho heigh-ho Heigh-ho heigh-ho

Ladies and Gentlemen!
I was just thinking the old pictures you've probably seen of people digging the tunnels for the original Northern line. There is one where there is something like twenty, thirty men, all standing near the tunnelling thing. And it just would be interesting to think if the current statistic of one in eight, or whatever it is... that there were men in that picture who were maybe struggling with something. Or perhaps they didn't struggle with it.

The temporary metal Haki stairs allowed us to descend from the street level at Montford Place into the site works below, footsteps clanging. The stairs were too narrow and too loud to allow us to chat, until we reached the bottom.

She said: Another anecdote, another memory. Because Irish miners, they are still thinking that Santa Barbara will protect them. And they always... in the whole project, they fix a small statue of thirty centimetres, in a box, with a light. And every day... it was just close to the Haki stairs going down the shaft... every day in their way to work, they pass, eh, close to the statue, Santa Barbara. And, and for them it is like a whole thing and they feel secure. Because she is protecting them.

So, yes, it has gone now. Because the excavation is finished and the main work is finished, and now it is installing the rails.

But, well, there always could be an accident, but the risk is obviously less than it was before than when you had the face open, and you can have the ground coming in.

As far as I know, we had two statues, one at Kennington Green and another one in Kennington Park.

We talked of their careers before becoming a Tube driver, from banking and IT support, to the hospitality industry. Once selected, initial training took place at Ashfield House, the setting for many stories.

He said: I was in the very early stages of a new relationship with somebody who is now my husband, and we were in The Black Cap cabaret bar in Camden. And it was a Sunday afternoon, and you get all the free magazines and papers there. Like the Pink Paper. And he opens it up, and he goes, look at that. And there was an ad in the Pink Paper for direct recruit drivers.

I still have the cut out of the ad.

Yeah. This is, for me, year eighteen or nineteen.

This was 2001, yeah.

We've not paid for a ticket in twenty years. It does trap you in those ways.

But I do believe it was, at the time, the first time the Underground had ever advertised for a direct recruit drivers. But they were really pushing for female drivers, and gay guys, if they were advertising in…

Because the money was incredible. I practically… it was double the salary that I was earning at the time, and at the time… both of us… he is still working for them, it was a company owned by <   >, which has now changed its name. It was greed. It was money and the holiday, and we lived in London, free travel, all the list of benefits from them.

So I said I'm going to go for this, and I went for it.

It was a complete culture shock. Apart from being at school, I'd never worn a uniform. I went to school in Ireland. Strict <   > school.

I was only one of four direct recruit drivers at Golders Green for a very long time. And three of us were gay. So there was me, <   > who has just retired and she is a lesbian, and <   >.

Morden… I think she moved house. Just put in a transfer.

She has gone up to Ashfield House. She was the Golders Green queen for arranging everything. And she still has a pink lottery going, which I'm a member of.

At the end of every year we go out and have a free night out. We will win it one day.

How many parties did we have at the Black Cap? We used to all be in the same corner. The Golders Green… by the window.

Til two, three years ago, it closed. We all… there were parties there. It is only ten minutes away. Just… if you finished work at eight o'clock.

> He said: Oh my God I'm dying! I need tea! I need tea! I need tea! I need tea! Put the kettle on! I know nothing! I know nothing! I come from Eee-tal-lee! I know nothing!

He said: <   > likes to come out with the gays, don't you?
He's been everywhere!

Ha ha ha

2/7/76 South London Press SOUTH LONDON PRE

Putting on the pub shine

THE NEWEST pub in the Covent Garden market, Nine Elms, got a shining official opening on Tuesday when the Pearly King and Queen of Islington came down, accompanied by a couple of Pearly troubadors, to parade their finery in the sunshine.

The Pearly King and Queen, Bill Cole and his sister Liz, opened the "Market Tavern" near the flower market.

For Liz, whose husband is Charles Sharm, it was a chance to inspect her husband's local, for he is a salesman in the flower market.

Pictured above are Bill and Liz—in Pearly knee-length trousers—doing a jig, accompanied by their minstrels, Ricky Conway and Steve Jones, outside the "Tavern."

The new pub has been open about two months but the official ceremony was postponed to coincide with the introduction of Wandsworth's local brew from Young's.

Unlike the other three pubs in the market area, the "Market Tavern," managed by George and Hilda Teed, is open during normal licensing hours as well as the 5 a.m. to 9 a.m. opening for the early-morning market workers.

heigh-ho Heigh-ho heigh-ho Heigh-ho heigh-ho Heigh-ho hum Heigh-ho heigh-ho it's

Ladies and Gentlemen!
As you were hanging off the back of the train, watching the platform, it would feel like someone was throwing sand into your face. You were basically in this cocktail of brake dust all the time.

Walking in the southbound tunnel, before our dinner at three am, we bumped into one of the supervisors of the miners who had dug out the areas that the tunnel boring machines could not reach.

He said: Oh, yeah. I would say so, yeah. They were from Manchester, and Yorkshire, and Newcastle. Yeah, they were from all round, like. We had a good few men here when we were doing the cross passages. Cos that was all hand dug.

Oh, it is better, yeah. Well the coal, you see, the coal would be… well, you do a lot on your knees, in their days, there would be a lot on their knees and digging and following the seams, you know, coal seams, so. Would have been hard work, like, at that time, years ago.

These are all a new generation.

Ah well they always end up going back and picking up some other type of work. They would probably follow you on some form of tunnel work, you know, maybe headings and connections and whatnot, smaller version of work, like. But they have to come here for the big one.

They do! But I wouldn't like to tell you what they sing!

No! They are rude, yeah. I won't tell you.

Tell him, I said <   > should know them himself!

Yeah, they would, though. They would. They'd have their own songs.

Those? I call them pig tails. But their real name are spring clips.

Ladies and Gentlemen!
In that moment it was like real mining work, because the space where we were working was really small. Maybe sometimes we were working a metre and a half by a metre. Eight people.

Golders Green and Morden are the largest train depots on the Northern line, in terms of driver numbers. Most of the managers are former drivers.

He said: And then when I was driving... because there is a beautiful acoustic in the Kennington loop... I would open up and sing into the tunnels, sometimes.

Oh, a mixture of things. Show tunes. I'm actually a choral trained singer. I'm in a church choir.

I've done some amazing things. I've been genuinely blessed. I've sung at Westminster Abbey, I've sung in the Royal Albert Hall.

Usually more baritone based songs, so like 'One Day More', Les Mis, or something you can kind of really get... an operatic, because the acoustic is so worth it.

And because no one is going to hear it, either.

I can do a Gregorian chant, now and again.

You used to. It is not as long now, but in the days of the old timetables which were under signals, you could literally be in the loop up to fourteen minutes, so that's a lot of time. And obviously you would open the door because you were not going to move anyway, and you would wait for your alarm to go off, or anything like that. And you would... ah...ahhh! Gave you something to do, you know what I mean?

I've been Northern the whole time I've worked for the company, funnily enough. So I became rostered at Euston and rostered at Tottenham Court Road. Tottenham Court Road was always known as the Pink Palace. Or has been for a number of years, not so much now. It was a very, very big majority of gay members of staff at the station. Very inclusive environment. Cos, you have to think, pre 2008 you had G.A.Y. right on top... there was a number of gay clubs around the Soho area. Soho was very gay.

Everyone was... you are obviously gay. The first day on the job. I have a colleague now, and she is one of my honorary mummies, and she said, you are gay, right? I went, I'm not? No, you must be. Well, haven't had sex with a man. Well,

we go Heigh-ho heigh-ho heigh-ho Heigh-ho heigh-ho it's One day more Another

I haven't had sex with a woman either. But, you know, and I was nineteen at the time. And I didn't know what I was.

No, no.

So we were always dealing with events. And then you had The Dominion with *We Will Rock You* which I know isn't a gay musical, but you know, you don't get any gayer than Freddie Mercury, bless him. Um, so to speak.

So I really did join a very, very inclusive and welcoming environment with men and women members of the LGBT community, and stuff like that.

It was just chance.

No, I think that has kind of gone away, but then the term pink depot has also gone away.

Yeah, cos, I mean, it is not that it is not spoken of. It's kind of, like, it is what it is.

In 2011 I applied to be an Olympic driver. Got that in 2011, started to become a driver in 2012. Passed out as a driver.

I got the Northern line. So I was very happy. Because I knew the stations, so all I had to focus on was the signals and the process of driving, so to speak, because we were still signals then. And then middle of 2013 I applied to be what was then a Duty Train Staff Manager. So what the current TM role is, but just desk based.

Got it. And I was actually based at East Finchley as a driver, so came over to Golders, which then became my nominated depot.

And I finally got through to be a Duty Manager. Was told I was going to be at Golders. But then my last day as a driver was a one under.

And this is where <   > and I come in, and the family thing.

Thankfully I was always looking for the next signal, so I didn't become stuck in the stop, start, open, close, stop, start, open, close.

I use my campness as a kind of disarming tool. Because I'm dealing with a lot of masculine, straight, in particular white, men, generally, who very much want you to know who is in control. And unfortunately, in this instance, you're the driver and I'm the Duty Manager... so there is an element which can be frictious.

So officially, um, we all get up to twenty drivers. But really I am a line manager to two hundred and something drivers here. And then I'm responsible for all of the drivers on the Northern line, so add another few hundred. But all direct management would then be sent to the local depot. But I might need to stand a driver down, or deal with them immediately. You deal with the extremes of emotions and it can be quite a lonely place, the Duty Manager. We see the worst of the worst. It is because of that we have to have a laugh. We have to have a support structure.

We have one hundred and six trains which are owned by Alstom, technically, of which we run a ninety-six train peak. So to put that in perspective, there are five hundred and something across the network, and we have ninety-six of them.

We are dealing with the old infrastructure that we have. Even though we have had modernisation, we are still not modernised. Not in every way. I mean you can see here, it isn't exactly modern! But you deal with what you have, you know.

I mean, I know it, cos I've heard a lot of the histories and I've been around the likes of <   > and stuff like that. <   > will answer the phone Golders Queen.

Yes. That phone. Golders Queen, how can I help you?

Oh it could be anybody. You really don't know who you are going to pick up the phone to.

If I'm working, and he is working, I'll sometimes pick it up and say Golders rainbow. Cos we are not green any more. We are every colour of the rainbow.

I never saw the purpose of Pride. I'm a different generation that doesn't necessarily need to express it. Because it just is what it is.

I mean, at the end of the day, now it is not like it is a royal crew, or anything like that. You are just... you are a driver.

Ladies and Gentlemen!
There is a beautiful acoustic in the Kennington loop…
I would open up and sing into the tunnels. Show tunes.

As the rail gang worked, at times we could barely hear each other above the noise, and through the earplugs. Lunch was at ten pm, and at that time the tunnels were almost silent, for an hour.

He said: That is the impact sound. With the impact gun, we will bolt the jigs to the rail. So we can, we are able to rise the level of the rail. And now… as soon as we finish marking, we are going to hear the drilling…the drill, drilling the rings.

But we are marking first, with the chalk.

February. And then we go to Nine Elms station. Here, we have started Nine Elms to Kennington. Battersea station is finished. And when we finish the running tunnels we go to Nine Elms station.

There is nothing about rails in Nine Elms. They need to fill up the station first. And then, once we finish the running tunnels, we go to Nine Elms. We can see from the beginning of this tunnel there is a door, a gate, but from the top of the gate we can see Nine Elms station, with nothing done.

I don't have the key. But I am tall enough to see on top of the gate.

What we are looking for them to do is fill up the concrete. The box is so low they need to fill it up to come with the rails. The rail level is like a couple of metres, concrete.

Well, I mean, this project… engineering is all about concrete, at the end of the day. Everything is all about concrete. Even for miners, who are thinking on London clay, the last stage is the concrete.

They do. They do. Sprayed concrete. At the end of the day they spray the concrete into the tunnels.

I am… they are always saying I love the concrete. Honestly, I like the smell of the concrete.

Probably. I mean there are so many things to add to the concrete, for example, this is... we can call this one C32, with fibres on it. The C32 means the strength of the concrete in a cubic or a cylinder. So when you make samples of the concrete, and you try to break it, the strength of the concrete to that, that test, is how you name the concrete. C32 means that 32 Megapascals is broken strength, that, yeah… and then you have the quality of the sealant. There are five

live when we are parted? One day more Tomorrow you'll be worlds away And yet with

qualities, one to five. You have chemicals to add, like any additive, like a retardant, accelerants to make it more fluid. They are so many types of concrete. The concrete for the miners is with steel fibres.

The day shift and the night shift. So, in the day shift there are fifteen guys. And in the night shift we are nine, ten guys, usually.

Well basically he is just, uh, kind of, uh, just making a noise like the song originally is. And they try to sing old songs from Spain, and not like recent ones. The typical song that you can listen from your grandparents.

The typical song that you can listen from your grandparents. Not the current songs.

Yeah, kind of traditional music from Spain. You know flamenco? Something like that. It is more flamenco songs, things that you can recognise.

He said: Juanjo!

He said: *¿Qué?* — What?

He said: *¿Cantas bien?* — Are you a good singer?

He sings: *Cántame, cántame por el camino* — Sing to me, sing to me on the way

He said: *Cántale un poquito, a dios. ¡A dios le canta!*
Sing a bit, to God. To God, sing it!

He sings: *Y a mi niña yo le canto, a mi niña yo le canto*
And I sing to my girl, to my girl I sing

Yo le canto — I sing to her

Lalalala mis penas — La la la all my troubles

Lala que es muy gitana — La la she is a real gypsy

Y a mi niña yo le canto — and I sing to my girl

He said: And that is the sound of pulling the clip. And there are some guys who are able to pull it at once, and some guys who need a small push with a key hammer to the green clip that you can see on the blocks. So the rail is clipped to the block with a green clip.

Yeah, well. Um. There's another thing. It looks like a churro. That thing that you eat in the morning, yeah? So looks like that. So we call it *churro.* And then the puller, we call them *churrella.*

Yeah, like the thing who make the churro. So it is like, eh, the Spanish words if I say to the guys like 'Install some clips' I will say 'Install some *churros* and take the *churella* with you somewhere'.

I don't know why we do these kinds of things. But yeah, it is a kind of like a green churro.

That's it. Depends on the country. Sugar is always there. There are plain ones and ones with the... but this depend on the recipe and person who make it. The ones here are plain ones!

I know the song he is singing now.

'Noches de bohemia y pasión'. But I don't know who, who...

I think, that one, I remember from Ketama, but I don't remember... originally it is not from them. It's another group. But.

From the 1990s, maybe?

Noches... de... bohemia... y pasión.

Yeah, about passion, yeah.

me cogiste de la mano, Yo iba Noches de bohemia y de ilusión Yo no me voy a la

Ladies and Gentlemen!
It just seemed like a concrete box. You had to go up
some stairs, concrete, and went in.

850,000 tons of 'muck' were extracted to create a space into which the line extension will go. By barge, the muck travelled from the pier at Battersea down to Essex, and was deposited at Goshems Farm, East Tilbury, raising up the land three metres higher than before. We strode down to the Thames there, in fluorescent yellow jackets.

She said: We are walking now on Northern line.

It will be agricultural. Whatever Mr Mott decides to do. But it would be nice to go down the River Thames, come out of London, and see some cows grazing. Because we are actually not that far from London.

It was poor farmland. It was in very poor condition. We've improved the condition… for recovery, the Environmental Agency want you to improve the condition.

It is waste because that person has finished with it, but it isn't really waste for us. Because we've used it to raise the ground and improve the land.

Clay, Thanet sand, alluvium. So they were the three types… chalk as well, in some places.

It all came here. The Northern line, it all came here. Except what went to the back-up site.

So there is Northern line here, and there is Northern line up here. Over there it is mixed with your Crossrail material.

And we are doing now the same as what we did back then… everything out of London down to Essex. All the material came from London in the Victorian times.

This is an old Victorian landfill. So, poor quality soils, lots of glass and the idea is to finish it all off, restore it, pass it back to the farmer so he can have it as agricultural and put his cows on there.

When we were doing Northern line, we were having three to four barges per day. And it was twenty-four hours, and it tidal, not seven til five, and then it is Saturday and Sunday as well.

Yes, yes, we've got the floodlights.

razón Como te olvidaste de eso Busco y no encuentro una explicación Solo la desilu-

Here is where the material comes in. That comes down by barge, pulled by a little tug… by GPS Marine. And then dock on to our old jetty. Then a long reach, you can just see the arm of the long reach, there, will unload the barge on to the back of a dumper and then the dumper will come along this Bailey bridge out and then go the tipping final destination. You've got phase 1, phase 2, phase 3, phase 4. And the majority of the Northern line was tipped in phase 3 and 4. And then that is tipped off by the dumper and then a blade will come and level it off. All the blades that we've got have got global positioning so they have all been utilised to do a certain level, which is three metres above ground.

We have the communication with the guys at the tunnelling end. So that we know that they're tunnelling… are they going to send a barge? Yes, they are. OK, we'll get our guys down here to work.

You will not get a barge load of 100% material. Some of the Northern line we have had bits of wood. So it might have hit the wharf. And it is deep down. Because London… the deeper you go in London the cleaner it supposed to get, but they, you can hit some peaty material as well. So we was getting a barge with a little bit of peaty material. And you know it is that just by looking at it at a distance. Because it is a slightly different colour, and then when you get, you touch it and you know it is peat. Just by look, and you think that's not London clay. Or that's not Northern line.

Just by looking at it. And the smell, as well.

Or you get a greeny colour. That is Thanet sand.

It is wet London clay. So they have added a drying out agent, to get it out of the tunnel, so get it so it is not just liquid. Because we are not allowed to take liquid material. It has to be in solid form. It had to be risk assessed, as we are near the water, we have got surface waters over there, so that material isn't going to react with any of the stuff already on.

We send that paperwork and everything to the Environment Agency. So they are aware that we are not just accepting clay, we are accepting clay mixed. They'll approve it, and then we can keep going.

The other day I saw two sea lions and that just goes to show that what we are doing is cleaning the river.

It is. Yeah, you can get a ferry from Tilbury docks.

Clay is… nothing gets through clay. So London weathered clay, or blue clay, brown clay, is solid. You can't get through it. You could make a clay little cup, fill it with water, go back the next day, and it would still be filled with water.

sión De que falsos fueron tus besos Ya no se como olvidarte Como arrancarte de mis

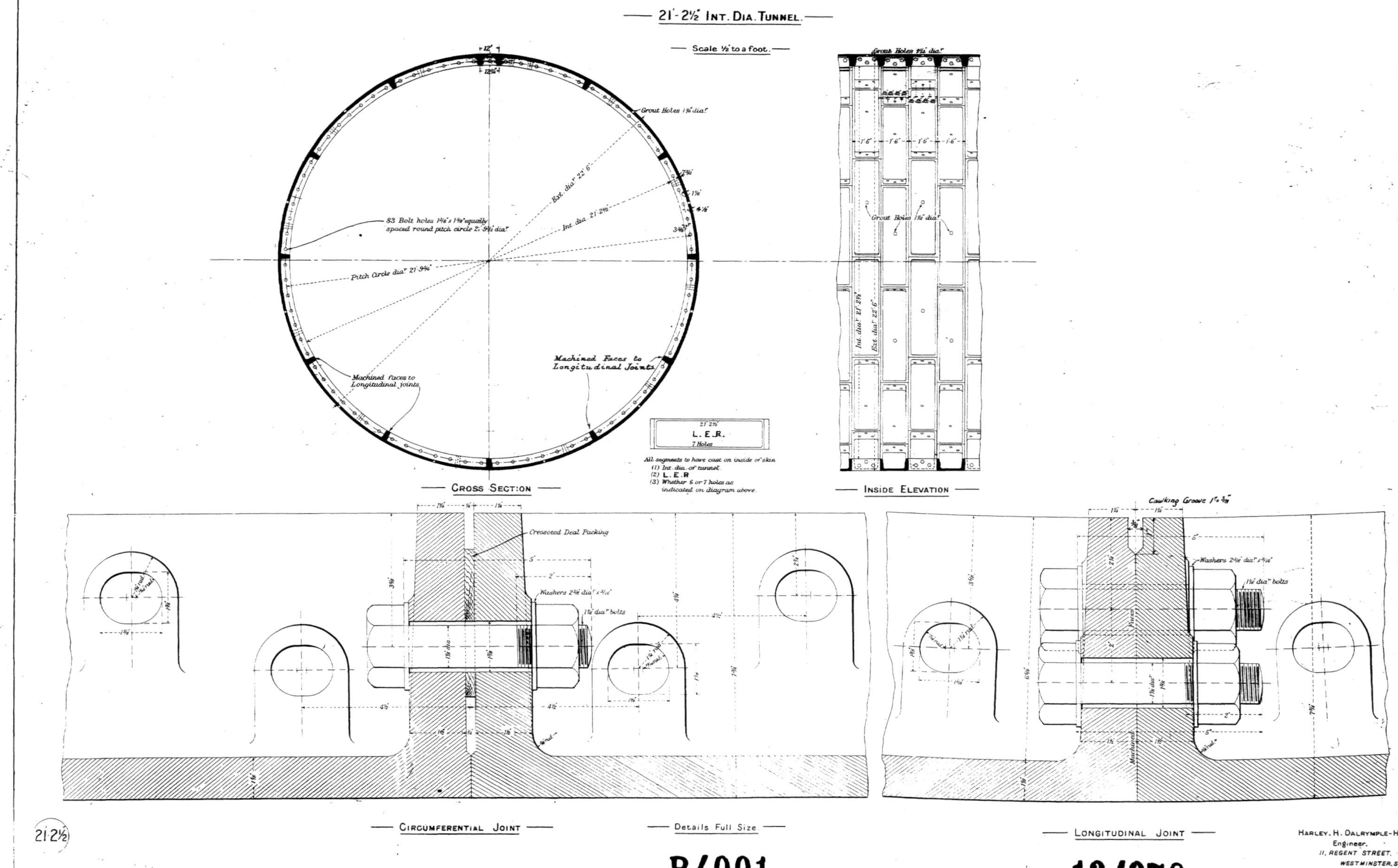

21'-2½" INT. DIA. TUNNEL.
Scale ½" to a foot.
Grout Holes 1⅜" dia.
83 Bolt holes 1⅛" x 1⅜" equally spaced round pitch circle 21'-9¼" dia.
Pitch Circle dia. 21'-9¼"
Ext. dia. 22'-6"
Int. dia. 21'-2½"
Machined Faces to Longitudinal Joints
Machined faces to Longitudinal joints
21'-2½"
L. E. R.
7 Holes
All segments to have cast on inside of skin
(1) Int. dia. of tunnel.
(2) L. E. R
(3) Whether 6 or 7 holes as indicated on diagram above.
CROSS SECTION
Int. dia. 21'-2½"
Ext. dia. 22'-6"
INSIDE ELEVATION
Creosoted Deal Packing
Washers 2⅜" dia. x 3/16"
1⅜" dia. bolts
Caulking Groove
Machined
Faces
CIRCUMFERENTIAL JOINT
Details Full Size
LONGITUDINAL JOINT
HARLEY. H. DALRYMPLE-HA
Engineer,
11, REGENT STREET,
WESTMINSTER, S.W.
21-2½
P/001
12/078
MICROBOX

If you try and do it with subsoil, subsoil doesn't compact. Clay does. But you have got to compact it, not have any gaps.

So we've put on subsoil, and they we're going to put top soil on top. Then you will leave it to Mother Nature… or Mr Mott, to do what he wants to do.

OK, so I started this about twenty years ago now. I started to do all the things to do with soils, and that's where I found it interesting. That is not just… there's a lot more to tipping a load of muck, as the lorry drivers would call it. It is the ground conditions, the ground water. It is the effect that all the soils have on our ground water. So I just started to do all the learning of the chemicals, the reactions that they have. The sulfates with the concrete, the concrete with the clay.

My Dad just thinks I work in mud. He said, I told you, you'd be, you'd work in mud. And I say, well it's not quite mud. It's not quite like that.

I come from Hungary, and it was a communist country. So I just got a one-way ticket to here.

I was nineteen, yeah. Didn't say to my Dad that it was a one-way ticket. I told my Mum that it was a one-way ticket, but she was aware that I was not coming back. But she was like, go for it, go for it. And you've got to… you can't, um… it's horrible here cos of the communist, um.

Probably stuck doing not a job, but being a mother to loads of children while my husband goes to work then goes to the pub. Not now. Not now. But Hungarian men… you were second class citizens. You wasn't in the position… but now you can. It is completely changed out there. But I remember I went back a couple of years after, and I went to my friend in the village and I said come on, let's go to the pub. And she said we can't go to the pub. It is full of men. And I went come on, we are going, going to the pub. So she said no, no, I can't. I went you do in England. You go to the pub. You drive a car. You work. So, yeah.

I've just painted a really bad picture of it. But at that time, '70s, '80s, so in that era, um, right up to 1989, cos I'd left by then. But I went back, I went back in 1990 for a holiday and that is when I saw the Russians leaving, as well. And that was quite sad, actually.

Worked in a bakery.

Stayed out of London, yeah.

I'm glad I'm in this industry. I couldn't work in supermarket with a load of women or just stacking the shelves or doing, you know, the cashier. Or working in accounts in the office. I'm glad I'm out there with the men, doing the work.

adentros   Desde que te marchaste   Mi vida es un tormento   Ya no quiero recordarte   Tan

So here, Northern line. You can see it.

Yes, slightly wetter. This area here hasn't been covered. You could take that back to Nine Elms and say I just thought I'd bring back some Northern line.

Yeah, three metres above Victorian waste. And it isn't ever going to come up through this clay. But if you hadn't have put clay on, and just put subsoil, eventually the rain would have brought things up.

Martina's was the Market Tavern's first night for women, beginning ten years before The Readers Wifes DJs arrived, with Duckie. Later there were other women's nights there, including KISS and COME.

She said: And on the right, you went into the room where Martina's used to be.

Ah, yes, there was a back bar with a pool table, a pinball machine. And plenty of seating and so that's where you went when you went to Martina's.

So maybe you came up those other steps? Cos you could come in that back way.

There was a lesbian comedy duo called Parker and Klein. They performed there. I thought Karen Parker was the sexiest thing imaginable. Ha, ha, ha. And you know we had discussions over who fancied Parker and who fancied Klein. That was at Martina's.

Well, I was really excited because it was really close to where I lived. And I think at the time you had to go up to North London to go up to dyke places, and er, this was right on my doorstep so I was thrilled. And I could walk across the roundabout. It was quite a big traffic, traffic going lots of ways, er… and at the time I had this grey cat that used to try to follow me across the roundabout. Because there was no bus garage, was there? There was just a great big roundabout. And he would follow me and I would have to shoo him back. So, he actually would be crossing the road at the roundabout and I'd have to tell him to go back. So I went when I could get rid of the cat, then, I'd go.

And yeah, Martina's it was wonderful. I'd never seen so many women together, in one spot at the time, indoors. It was great.

Yeah, it was very busy. Especially the first night was very busy. I think every dyke, or interested dyke, you know what you call a *dyke-curious* woman, in South London, turned up and their mates from North London came too. It was pretty packed.

I suppose it felt like home, was the main difference. It did have the feeling sometimes in North London that it was a bit more mainstream. Um. And…

oh yes, one thing I remember about the Duke of Wellington in North London is that there were various faction disputes going on there. And I was joking with a friend saying it should be like, it should have the doors like in a Western.

Every so often there would be special DJ there and, you know, like Vivacious and you know, it was all systems go.

And another thing was that Martina's was on a Monday night. It was on every Monday and I went every week.

It must have been 1985, '86, yeah.

It was very political. It was incredibly political. Because we were so harassed. We were constantly harassed. We had no legal protection. We could lose our houses, our jobs, our kids. All those things were real, you know.

Yes, it was before Clause 28. It was the miners.

Yeah, and we always had a march to go to, or… you know.

distante De todo aquello que era nuestro Pero el aire me trae Aromas de recuerdo No

Ladies and Gentlemen!
There wasn't any white lighting, it was all either red, green or purple. Depending on what outfit you wore, it looked bleeding awful. If you were wearing like green combats and a red light, it didn't look very good.

We spoke of all the mines in which he had worked, before he became Head of Tunnelling and had taken charge, here.

1983 Park Mill Colliery (closed 1989)
1989 Riccall Mine (closed 2002)
1995 Whitemoor Mine (closed 2001)
1996 Kellingley Colliery (closed 2014)
2002 Harworth Colliery (closed 2008)
2002 Daw Mill Colliery (closed 2012)
2011 Newlands Mine, Australia
2013 Oaky Creek Mine, Australia
2014 Northern Line Extension

He said: So at the moment we are underground on the new Northern Line Extension tunnels. We are underneath Kennington, about half a kilometre from Kennington Station, or a third of a mile from Kennington station. We are about seventeen or eighteen metres underground, and we are just short of the new step plate junction that we constructed as part of the Northern Line Extension project works, where the existing Northern line has been connected into from the new Northern line.

We are stood in a tunnel that was created by a sprayed concrete lining method. Er, we dug this tunnel in early 2017, and we have since put a secondary lining of cast in situ concrete to create a permanent lining tunnel. We have also installed the railway track and connected it to the Northern line which we did in a blockade at Christmas 2017.

So we are stood in a tunnel. The tunnel is 5.2 metres internal diameter. There is an invert pour of concrete, to make sure the rail is on a flat surface. I can see railway track, looking down, towards the shaft and back up towards the trains, and in the background you can hear one of the Northern line trains coming around Kennington Loop, as it heads on its journey back Northbound through Charing Cross towards Edgware or High Barnet. I can also see all the cable, CMS… cable management system, brackets, where the permanent cables will be installed. I can also see some tunnel lighting. We've got an invert where it catches water, any water comes into the tunnel. And we have got firefighting equipment and some electrical distribution equipment and a first aid box. All within proximity of where I am standing.

me pidas que me calle Y tu no sabes lo que siento Me has hecho una herida En mis sen-

My responsibility for TfL was for the whole of the tunnelling works for the Northern Line Extension. That included the two shafts at Kennington Park and Kennington Green, all the tunnels, the tunnel boring machine, all the spray concrete linings, and all the extensive hand tunnelling and timber headings which we did, and all the associated ground works. It included utility diversions. It included extensive piling. And it included some work in other utilities such as Thames Water, Southwest storm sewer, etc., where we had to carry out remedial works prior to tunnelling. It also includes all the ground monitoring and de-watering across the project, to enable the tunnelling work to take place.

I left school just aged sixteen, and after a short period working in an archive office in West Yorkshire, I started working in the coal mining industry. I was one of the, er, the last entrants before they cut recruitment. I was still a teenager in the great miner's strike of 1984, which was an experience I'll never forget. Er, and my only regret is that I didn't have a camera and photograph some of the things that I saw, because some of the things I saw were almost, almost unexplainable or unbelievable. The amount of social upheaval and change that I saw in what was clearly a critical moment in British industry. I then worked for a coal miner for ten years, on coal facings, headings and hard rock headings. And then I progressed as a mine deputy. I became a chartered mining engineer.

I think the engineering marvel is that when we came up to the existing Northern line with our spray concrete tunnels, we basically reached a cast iron tunnel, that was one hundred years old, with trains running through it. And we mined up alongside that cast iron tunnel, for seventy, eighty metres. We then mined over the top of it, all with sprayed concrete. But then we came out and we mined below it, so this cast iron tunnel was at the side of our tunnel. And then we went in with a series of tipper headings and dug underneath it, in seventeen, eighteen locations... little tunnels, to go underneath the Northern line. And each time we pulled out one of those tunnels, we filled it with reinforcement, and concrete, to support that tunnel. And then we dug up, by hand, round the blind side of that tunnel. So we ended up, at the end of it, with a seventy-metre long excavation with a railway tunnel made of cast iron running through the middle of it, supported by ropes and various temporary works, and stanchions and, and steelwork, and trains were running through this. And all through this, we worked in two locations simultaneously. We carried it out. We did it on target. We did it safely, with virtually no accidents, no injuries. And we never disrupted a single train for the travelling public while we did it. So that is what makes it to me an engineering marvel. And a real marker of teamwork, and success.

Several regulars talked of walking through the petrol station to reach the Towers. The barman also remembered the rooms below. We sat outside, at his garden table, just one postcode away.

He said: The building was… to me it is very recognisable, but it was pretty unprepossessing. It was a mixture of concrete and dark glass. It was almost black glass, and slightly creamy concrete. Just your normal skyscraper. The Market Tavern was on the first floor of it. Or, no, I think it was a floating building. I don't think it went down to the ground. Did it? Oh yes, it must have done. That was our cellar. We had our cellar on the ground floor. And then The Market was on the first floor. And we took up the whole, the whole floor of our section of the skyscraper. And I think it might have had more than one section, the skyscraper.

That's right. The entrance we went in was off, it was off, um, it was off, what what was it, Wandsworth Road? So if you come in from Clapham you come past Sainsbury's, which has moved around its site. But was still on that site, then. And then there was a petrol station alongside of which was the entrance to the flower market. And a bit further on the entrance to the Market Tavern was a flight of stairs, concrete stairs, going up to a very plain set of black double doors which would have been open or shut, and the arched thing around the other side, that was the entrance to another club.

I've got no idea. I never went. There was another entrance to The Market, though. I can't believe you've never been there. I mean, that's so weird!

So our door, the orientation… the building wasn't square on to any road, really. So our stairs went up, facing Wandsworth Road, basically, on the left hand corner, if you stood on Wandsworth Road and looked at it, the front left hand corner there were stairs up. And that was our main door.

It was beer called Colt 45, Holsten Pils… these were cans… and Red Stripe. We sold Beamish.

There was a night which was very much not leather. It was probably then called vanilla. It was called Jimmy Dean's… someone will remember. That was… I think it was men and women. It was a lot more racially diverse. And I think it was more fashionable music.

Ladies and Gentlemen!
Standing in the door of the Pink Flam-ing-o… cry-ing in the rain… Du du du du… du du du… It was a kind of so-so love… and I'm gon-na-make sure it never happens ag-a-in… Me and thee… it had to be… the standing joke of the year… You were a sleep around… ur, lost and found… and not for me I fear… Du du du du, du du du…

We sat in the canteen. For the Historic Trackwalk, she chose 'House of the Rising Sun' by The Animals, and 'Computer Blue' by Prince. The first, because it was significant to her and her wife.

She said: So when I get to Kennington, get everyone off the train, close the doors. I now have the option of doing a positive action and the train drives me though manually. There is a stopping point, it's called a pseudo platform, in the middle of the tunnel. It is basically just to set the system from Southbound to Northbound.

Because you are going in and basically making a U-turn. If I was going to drive in manual, I would flick the switch on the right hand side. The big red one. Flick it over one notch from automatic to PM, Protected Manual.

Protected Manual is just what it says. It is manual driving, but you are protected by the rules and the computer system. Meaning if something goes wrong, your train will stop. So while you are in Protected Manual your computer system knows where you are and what you're are doing. For you to drive the train, you use the Manual handle.

Again, two actions. The computer system, and the handle. If then something happens to you, the computer will pick that up. And if you drop the handle, it's OPO, one person operation, drop the handle, the thing automatically brakes. So…

So, according to them, the powers that be, the reason why you are supposed to drive manually, is that if something happens to you in the tunnel, they know about it.

But that's the thing, the train stops anyway, at the pseudo platform.

And then you have to start it up again, that's the thing.

So whether you drive manually, or not manually, if something is going to happen, you are still going to be in a tunnel.

besos   Ya no se como   There is a house in New Orleans   They call the Rising Sun   And

Ladies and Gentlemen!
I think that was the last bit that they
demolished was the steps up to it.

The Market Towers were slender, but not quite minimalist, because that came later. Maybe the style of Mies van der Rohe had influenced GMW's tower buildings at the time, judging by the others that still exist in London. In the original feasibility study there had been a proposal for a railhead to serve the Markets.

He said: All I can remember of the Market Tavern… I have a vision of cherry red. And chintz.

To be honest, it kind of wasn't the done thing for the project architect to go and get blethered in one of the local… whatevers. I remember the QS's in those days used to wear bowler hats. So at the very least we would have worn ties.

So originally the Market Towers was designed to have a piled foundation, going down, ooh, twenty plus meters. But having just taken over as project architect… and in those days the site was huge… if you can imagine forty people round the table. Because all the subcontractors would come along. I was back in the office one day and I get a phone call from the site. And it goes something like 'ere gov, we've got a problem. You know all these piles, yeah, well a pile is supposed to take five cubics of concrete. We have just put five ready mix lorries down there and that is twenty-five cubics. And we can't see the concrete. So I phoned the engineer and said, site, now. I drove down to London. And I'm looking down a hole which is empty. And said stop the job. Rethink. We can only have found something. Well it transpired, if you think back to aged London, little streams find their way into the river. Little streams became open sewers, and then they were bricked over, typically only over, not over and under.

The pile had hit an underground stream. So we were about the fill the Thames with concrete. We had been doing so for several weeks, if not months or years.

So I think that central portion when the tower buildings were, but not the podium, was a raft eight feet thick, reinforced concrete.

Not essential where you have got good bearing capacity, but bear in mind that the river's moved around. Often half a mile each way. So you have a lot of silt and sand built up there. And therefore poor bearing capacity.

It was an Act of Parliament because it was national infrastructure, the transfer from Covent Garden to Nine Elms.

It was 1973. I would have been twenty-five.

it's been the ruin of many a poor boy   And God I know I'm one   My mother was a tailor   She

I even remember the project number. The project number was 361.

Oh yeah. All my mates at university wanted to see it. It was the biggest project in the UK and I was running it. So they'd come and stay overnight.

The building was twin towers, but sixteen and twenty-two stories of occupied floors, probably another two above that. Slipped H, twin towers, one higher than the other. Classic towers on a podium, with a link to the Market, and a substructure.

The boundary went through Market Towers. That way, across from Wandsworth Road to Nine Elms Lane. And this bit only was Lambeth. All the rest was Wandsworth. And the boundary was modified when the project was completed. Which was fine, but it meant we had appease two local authorities.

So I graduated in '71. The project had been designed and gained its Act of Parliament, and I joined a team which was essentially four teams in one, to run the Market. So there was a team doing fruit and veg, a team doing flower, a team doing Market Towers and then a team doing all of the externals, the entrances, the roads, the bridges, the boundary walls.

So the bridge that linked the Flower Market comes off the first floor of the Flower Market, and there it is. And that's a bit of it.

Bronze glass. In architectural terms is it bronze glass. Bronze tinted glass, and the curtain walling is bronze anodised aluminium. So these, here, this is all in situ concrete.

So if we start with the concrete. This is sand blasted, in situ, ribbed, ribbed, R-I-B-B-E-D, concrete. So the way this would work would be they would… when you pour concrete, you have a shuttering, OK, which is a board, and this case it was marine ply. And it would be oiled and the reason for the oil is so that the concrete doesn't stick to the wood.

Yeah. And then you had little sort of wooden fillings. And enlarged, they are sort of trapezoidal. OK?

It's a lot easier to get out. But it also means you get the reverse of that in the concrete. So that is your rib.

The ribs would have been between fifty and seventy-five mils, two and three inches

Yeah quite thin. But you could put your fist in.

sewed my new blue jeans My father was a gamblin' man Down in New Orleans Now the

Um, it was becoming popular. It became very popular with buildings like this. Because it keeps its colour fairly well. In this case we didn't put any special colour agents in the concrete. It was just too expensive. But, you get the colour from the aggregate. And I always, I always tell people making concrete is like life. The aggregate needs to have big solid chunks of stone. Little bits of sand and cement, that fill the gaps. And then there is the cement which is the glue that holds it together. So that is your concrete.

So these vertical elements, now these horizontal striations… another word for you… are fair faced. And they are there to represent the floors.

So sandblasted, ribbed, insulate concrete, curtain wall. All of this stuff, and the cladding for the bridge and the podium, aluminium curtain wall, spandrel panels, bronze anodised… bronze glass.

No, an acidic vat, and you pass electric currents through it. And the electrodes change the colour from natural, silver and the natural one is called mill finished. Mill as in steel mill. M-I-L-L. And that was produced by Crittall.

There were not too many buildings of this height in London. We needed it to be wind tested. That's fine, but in this country, when you get the highest wind, you tend to get rain, and there was no standard for wind and water testing simultaneously. Nor was there any machinery to do it with. So we got Crittall to take their panels to a place where there was an aero engine. Whilst the wind was blowing we poured concrete. And watched to see if there was any leakage. But the requirement we had was to resist gust force in the Thames corridor of a hundred and four miles an hour.

This wasn't an air conditioned building. It was cooled and it was heated. But it had no humidity.

The Market Towers wasn't even open when the Queen opened the Market.

Because it was, I think because of the Act of Parliament, they had to open on that day.

My role in that particular day was, um… cos it was Queen, Prince Phillip and Fred Peart, who was the Minister for Agriculture. And the hierarchy was Covent Garden Market Authority, DEFRA… these days, but it was something else then… Treasury, government.

Because it was royal, and because it was still a building site, because Market Towers wasn't complete, um, we had the police and the dog teams there all night. You know what it is like. You are on a construction site, the first thing you are aware of is dust and cement, and all sorts in the air. So the poor dogs can't work normal time spans. Much reduced. So we needed break times. And I remember I accompanied, as much as anything to show them there where things were.

All night. I then got changed, and found a tie, went off, and had a glass of champagne.

Many of the men still working in the Flower Market told me it was all a very long time ago.

He said: I give up drinking in '76. I went to get people out of there. The last time I went up there I went and got <   > out. And he's been gone a while.

Dead. They are nearly all dead.

There were three <   >s, dad, son, grandad. And he'd say go and get him! And I'd say, I'll go and get him.

No, a lot earlier than that. <   > would live his life in there. He was a right old lush. And play cards. But they all know me up there. Because I was up there so much. I got people out of there.

Yeah, I'd arrive. They'd say who's on the way home?

There was always music in the background, always. I'd be fibbing if I said I could access that. But we had that open jukebox style of thing up there. Like, yeah. If you can access that from back in the day you are pretty well solid.

Mid 1970s stuff… don't think anyone played any punk up there.

We spoke on Skype, as he now lives in Amsterdam. The photos of him are at the Bishopsgate Institute, in the archive.

It was also known as the pansy depot. Before I'd even got to Parsons Green, when I was doing my training, at White City… in the 1959 stock, behind the driver's head there is a little recess in the cab. It looks like a little niche into which a statue ought to go, or something like that. It has no purpose whatsoever. It is one of those strange design quirks. And I very camply said, when I was being trained… oh, look, you've got a lovely little niche for a vase of flowers here! And he said, you are going to Parsons Green, I suppose.

For me, 1974 to 1979. What was useful for me was it gave me money to fuel my activism. I was living in Brixton squats at the time.

The mess room was on the up platform, the platform going into town, half way down, and effectively it was only a two story annex building on the side, actually on the platform. And the downstairs was the roster room and all the rest of it, and the upstairs was the canteen. But it wasn't like a big canteen, you know what I mean? It was an outlier depot, so it was you know, forty, fifty foot-long by twenty foot wide.

Yeah, well the interior was standard, er, LT brown anthracite floor, tiling up two thirds of the wall, and then more of that sort of anthracite and 1930s style steel casement windows. Little strip windows. And of course the main canteen was at Earl's Court.

It was all male, number one. And number two, an incredible number of ex services people. Ex-forces. And yes, there were a huge number of quite closeted gay men, who were never outed by the rest of us, which I think is quite interesting. People just got on with it. Yes, there were closet cases, you know. The <   >, at the time. And his boyfriend. But we never outed them. But if you were out there, then you were very very out and it was a question of… we wandered into canteens between Acton Town and Earl's Court, and Barking and Upminster… Ah, hello girls, how are we all today? You know. Ha ha ha. Looking a bit down in the dumps, darling!

Well it rubbed off to a certain extent. And maybe this is the part of the ex-forces, but the minute you had been accepted by the people in your depot you got stood up for. So there was that kind of thing going on.

It started as a bit of joke, egged on by my driver, <   >. And so I'd put in this thing that I ought to be able to wear all the uniform that was appropriate to my grade.

Guard, yes. And the Czechoslovakian serge trousers that they gave us was pulling all the hair off the back of my legs, it was really… well, if I wanted to Immac I would, thank you very much. And why couldn't I wear a jaunty little side cap, etc. etc. etc. So this went through all the chain of command. You know this is not x and y and z. And it also got taken up by the local ASLEF branch, as well. So I became the first out gay ASLEF delegate to a gay workers' conference that happened in Leeds '76 or '77.

Eventually I got summoned to 55 Broadway. And in 55 Broadway there was a whole row of like, people with huge amounts of braid, sitting on one side of the table, with a little person sitting at the edge of the table, who was a psychiatrist, who said you do realise, <   >, that, if you *did* have a sex change, we would give you a year off, while you sort it all out. We would hold your job open. You would retain your pension rights. And you could come back to work for us. So in some ways they were being really sweet. They were being really nice. And… you do know we have a few people who have had sex changes working for us, you know, so you wouldn't be alone, even on your line… there is the ticket inspector in… But I said that is not the point. That is *really* not the point.

So then I and <   >, now dead, faxed it out to anybody and everybody, saying this is the story. Saying tomorrow is my last day of work, and the reason I will be resigning, and I will be on London Transport Earl's Court station doing my last day as a Tube guard in a female guard's uniform. So we got there, and we had Time Out, Gay News, The Standard, Reuters, The Guardian. We had about eight stringers. It was November 1979.

And we got to Earl's Court station and the station was an absolute commotion, all these people in braid and all the rest of it. And all the trains that were going across back and forth from Earl's Court all giving me the thumbs up and the beep. And allowing me to pose on the back of their trains, to do this, which was totally *not* allowed. And somewhere there is actually a picture of the woman, lovely girl, <   >, platform attendant, who lent me her costume… or gave it to me, to do the whole thing. But the photos are all very accessible

Yes.

You could tell if you were fit to go in by the number of stairs you had to walk up to get into it. Because it was on a podium, and that podium was up three flights of unforgiving concrete stairs. And then you went into the Market Tavern, which was a boozer, looking like it was part of a 1970s tower block, which it was. Which had one long bar at the front with a stage, where Lily used to perform. Miss Savage… well into the 1980s.

Drag queens used to do the circuit. And I always remember she used to do Body Positive benefits. She'd say fucking hell, get your fucking tired arse off this fucking stage. Right. My God, here we are. There's another twenty-seven bloody bingo prizes I've got to give out, because you are all going to bloody… we are all going to bloody die soon, so you have all got to have a bloody present. Ha ha. Gallows humour. Greatly appreciated, you know. And that was the front bar. I know it opened for the Market traders, and if you were known, then you could get in.

I remember meeting the Market traders, and later people like John Conteh, and Alex Higgins. And various East end and South London villains.

The back bar was officially the traders' bar, so you were privileged if you got in.

My favourite thing on the duke box was 'Poetry in Motion'. You know 'Poetry in Motion'? And I used to put that on the minute I used to go in there. Because they still had one of those old fashioned duke boxes, where you could actually put money into it. And lots of things by Dusty, you know?

We did used to camp it up occasionally. I mean, we used to arrive in Earl's Court and do the announcements, you know, please get out at the rear end, by my guard. Or at the stations… this one for The Colherne, you know. Or… we have arrived in the gay capital of the west!

And of course there was the thing at the time that the carriage before last, right, was the gay carriage.

Oh yes. And that was suggested in various gay newspapers, in terms of it being a safety issue.

During their current shifts, we exchanged tales of distinctive places on the Northern line, to be encountered, perhaps, from their cabs.

He said: What about gay ghosts on the Northern line… because I did a reverse move this afternoon, into Tooting Broadway. And there is lots of these stories about people hearing things, in Tooting and the southern part of the line, isn't it? From Kennington and Oval, isn't it? There is a lot of ghost history there. I didn't feel at ease.

Well, it is usually men who are spotted, according to these stories.

my side Her lovely locomotion keeps my eyes open wide Poetry in motion see her gentle

Ladies and Gentlemen!
Engineering is all about concrete, at the end of the day.
Everything is all about concrete. Even miners, who are
thinking on London clay, the last stage is the concrete.

A group of us talked.

She said: I think it felt like it was in the middle of nowhere.

She said: Yes, that's true.

She said: You approached it, and it seemed quite bare all around it.

She said: Cos you had that little walk from the Underground and you didn't quite know where you were going. And then, there it was, and you went up the steps.

She said: It was the only place you ever went up the steps to, wasn't it?

sway A wave out on the ocean could never move that way I love every movement There's

Ladies and Gentlemen!
We have started Nine Elms to Kennington.
Battersea station is finished. And when we finish
the running tunnels we go to Nine Elms station.

nothing I would change **She doesn't need improvement** She's much too nice to rearrange

HAMBURG SÜD

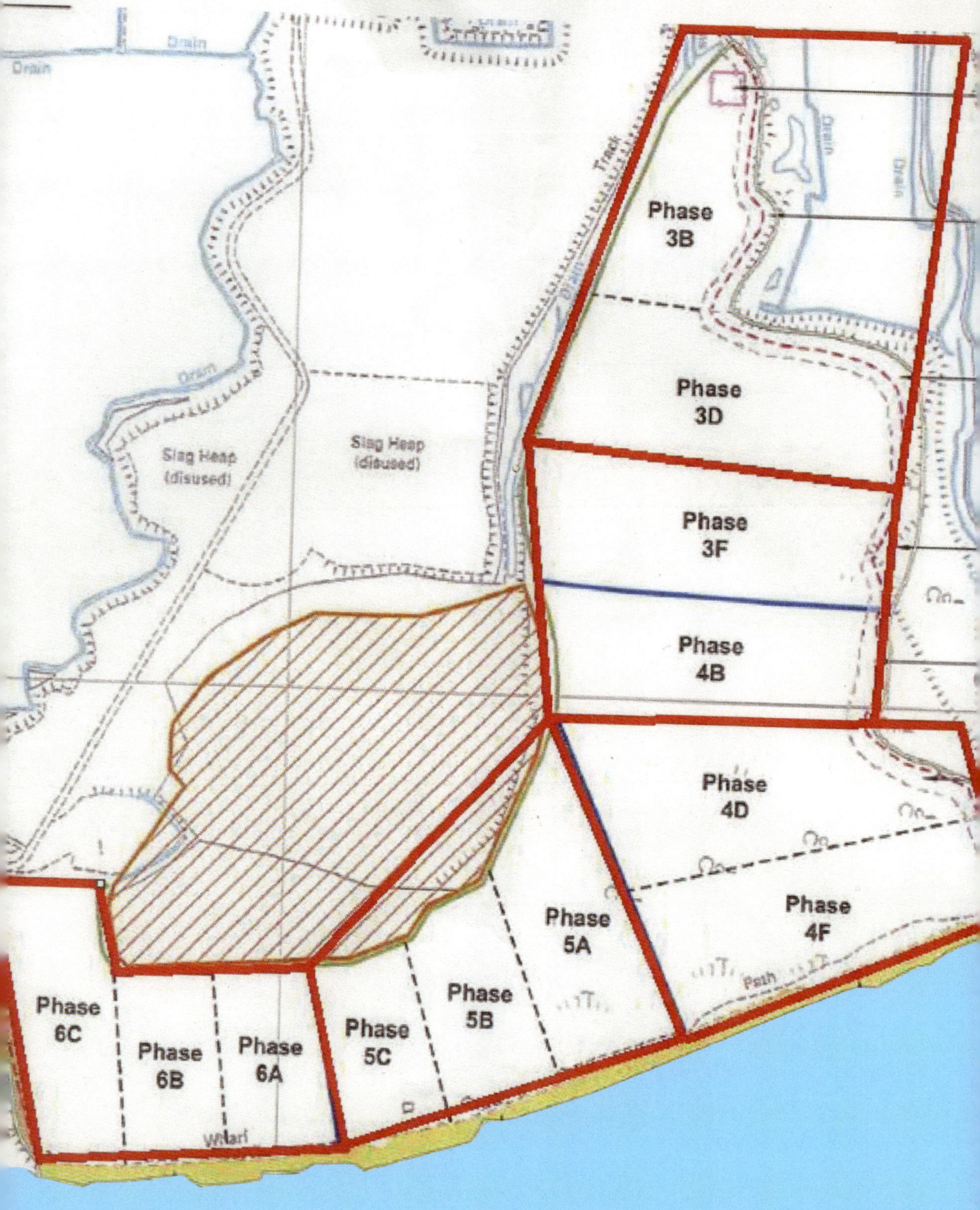

Drain
Drain
Track
Drain
Drain
Drain
Phase 3B
Phase 3D
Slag Heap (disused)
Slag Heap (disused)
Phase 3F
Phase 4B
Phase 4D
Phase 4F
Phase 5A
Phase 5B
Phase 5C
Phase 6A
Phase 6B
Phase 6C
Path
Wharf

UNDERGROUND
SANCTUARY.
"'Tis pleasant, through the loopholes of retreat,
To peep at such a world; to see the stir
Of the great Babel, and not feel the crowd;
To hear the roar she sends through all her gates
At a safe distance, where the dying sound
Falls a soft murmur on th' uninjured ear."
William Cowper.
J.R. & Co. Ltd
THE SOONEST REACHED AT ANY TIME
GOLDERS GREEN
(HENDON AND FINCHLEY)
A PLACE OF DELIGHTFUL PROSPECTS

Remember that I cannot say everything

A few months into this two-year project, I spent a morning in the tunnels re-speaking and singing some of the material that I had been accumulating. I was accompanied by local drag artist King Frankie Sinatra, who had run a club at the Market Tavern, and we took down speakers and a turntable on which I blasted out a single remembered by a barman. During the performance, King Frankie added her MC announcements of the time, and the Head of Tunnelling surprised us with his extensive knowledge of Queen's Greatest Hits, as did the official Northern Line Extension photographer. Later I edited down the audio recording of the event to ten minutes, and played it for the public at a temporary gallery at Riverlight on Nine Elms Lane.

Remember that I might be overheard

I had not foreseen the capacity of the tunnels as resonant acoustic chambers, the distance that sound would carry, or how it would startle visitors from senior management, who heard the thudding beat and vocals 'I've got the power' between the drilling, hammering and movement of plant machinery, and approached to see what was going on. I'm not sure what he said – I found indecipherable murmurs on the audio recording – but the Head of Tunnelling placated the onlookers, and afterwards the incident became one of our favourite anecdotes when people enquired about the project, and the performances down the tunnels.

Remember not to take my breathing for granted

Several levels down, at the tally hut, I strapped to my waist the metal tin of liquid oxygen, exchanging my passport for a small numbered brass disc, before descending further. Miners never take their air for granted. For the older Northern line drivers, who had been guards, breathing on the job was associated with inhaling brake dust and the taste of resin and iron. At the Flower Market these days, the air is temperature controlled and delicately scented, if you are not desensitised after years of working there.

Remember that all bodies are signals

A year on from the excavation with hand tools, it was easy to forget that for many months the work and culture of miners had dominated, including digging beside each other in hot, confined spaces. On a day trip to one of his former pits in South Yorkshire, bars of green soap displayed in a cabinet and with P.H.B. pressed into them prompted the Head of Tunnelling to tell me about men in lines, at the end of their shift, washing each other's backs. In the new tunnels, I have not yet managed to persuade anyone to share with me the more explicit lyrics sung down there. Maybe that would be different if I were a man.

Remember that I am not the only one making sounds
We made our way along the running tunnel towards the first cross passage, away from the loudest drilling and grinding. Subsequently, in common with the shift engineers, I became able to distinguish the distinctive clangs of various bolts, and the rhythms of bangs, creaks and rumbles as the long welded rail was fitted, and fixed with the clips. The loudest, harshest sound was the trimming of the rails, producing offcut sections which clinked into white waste bags. And amongst all this activity were repeated fragments of old Spanish 'grandparent' songs, sung or whistled through the night, when the track team had the tunnels almost to themselves.

Remember the snags between listening and repeating
Before I transcribed them, the voices that I had accumulated lived in my headphones and as sound waves on an editing screen, and were released as I re-spoke them into the tunnels. Trying to repeat voices heard through an earpiece often made me stumble, as questions, responses, anecdotes and banter advanced faster than I could process them. Afterwards I began to type out the words of the engineers and rail 'gangs', as well as the architect, flower sellers, market porters, lesbian and gay DJs, Northern line Tube drivers... Some of them overlapped in the Market Tavern, back in the day. Others will drive passengers along the new track.

McALPINE
HADEN YOUNG
BUILDING SERVICES ENGINEERS
HADEN YOUNG
HADEN YOUNG

Car park
Wandsworth
Lambeth Bridge
Waterloo

Banco
Español
Londres

THE NEW COVENT GARDEN MARKET

we shall be there...

...and remain here.

From the new branch we shall be able to transact business direct with any commercial centre, be it as big as New York, Madrid, Paris or Brussels or as small as Abarán, Burriana, Gandía, etc.

be LONDRES

BANCO ESPAÑOL EN LONDRES

(*Limited Liability Company Incorporated in Spain*)

FIVE Branches in London and Liverpool.
AFFILIATED TO: BANCO EXTERIOR DE ESPAÑA, MADRID
ASSOCIATE BANKS IN: France, Belgium, Germany, Morrocco.

MARKET TAVER
FREE HOUSE
COURAGE

MARKET TAVERN
COURAGE

RAIL DRAWINGS
DRAWINGS
MEP
FIT OUT
& RAILS

B4-08
Train Crew
Tea Point

The Tunnels Team Tea Making Guide

Is that tea or did you scoop it out a muddy puddle? (MT) - 3 bags, 3 minutes and plenty of stirring

The killer whale likes it sweet.
1 bag 1 minute and 1 sweetener.

The monomash (JD) – 30 second dunk, minimal stirring

It looks like milk (JC) the quick dunk
GIRLPOWER!

'Give tube drivers ... we'll ballot for str...

by SAMANTHA BOOTH

TUBE drivers are demanding ear defenders when travelling through loud stretches of the London Underground system.

Trade union Aslef says it has made it "very clear" to management at Transport for London (TfL) that if they did not deal with the situation there will be "no option other than to ballot for industrial action".

The *Tribune* revealed earlier this year how Northern line passengers were being exposed to noise equivalent in volume to a live rock concert.

Passengers are sometimes seen covering their ears on a section of track between Tufnell Park and Euston, while there are also noise issues on stretches of the Victoria, Jubilee and Central lines.

Noise is forcing some tube drivers to reduce speed

TfL says the noise levels are within Health and Safety Executive (HSE) regulations, but have been providing drivers with ear plugs.

After six months of discussions, Aslef is now demanding drivers are given ear defenders, which go over the head and cover the entire ear.

TfL says it is reviewing the need for and type of ear protection. Aslef says a system, called Pandrol Vanguard, was installed to help reduce noise in homes above tracks but has increased the din in tunnels.

Now, some drivers are choosing to reduce speed in these areas.

One driver, according to Aslef, said: "The noise levels between Kentish [Town] and Euston are beyond anything I can describe. You can't hear a radio message at all."

Aslef said: "London Underground has consistently stated that noise levels are within 'legal limits' a
provide
tion, suc
for driv
problem
found."

The
issue w
ground'
last Thu
ear def
ers on a

"Som
drive at
these '
areas,"
added.
the ful
union i
their he

"Lon
has sai
setting
to deal
advised
too late
shop a

ar defenders or ke action' – union

using to
protec-
efenders
igate the
can be

sed the
Under-
of safety
manding
all driv-
es.
hoose to
speed in
anguard'
tatement
ill have
of this
protect
ifety.
erground
nsidering
ng group
ssue. We
it it was
er talking
ded that

they act now." Aslef has asked TfL to respond by next Friday.

"If Underground management are not prepared to act to protect the safety of our members, then we will not hesitate to do what is needed," it has warned.

TfL, which says it regularly monitors noise levels, maintains HSE guidance suggests tube noise is highly unlikely to cause any long-term damage to the hearing of staff and customers. It said noise limits set out by HSE are based on exposure over an eight-hour period.

A TfL spokeswoman said: "Following a Health and Safety Forum with unions, we are reviewing the need for and type of ear protection offered to train operators. We have agreed to feedback to the unions shortly on our findings and will, of course, make any changes that are necessary."

TALK FOR HEALTH

Do You Need To Talk?

Free Programme in Talking for Wellbeing

The **FREE** Talk for Health Tasters and Full Programmes enable wellbeing and good relationships by teaching:

- Honest talking – being the real you
- Empathic listening
- Basic counselling skills
- A clear structure for ongoing groups

You'll gain access to Talk for Health Cafes plus ongoing groups and events to continue building your wellbeing.

Taster July 11th

Next Full Programme starts September

"Enjoyable, inspiring, safe, supportive, liberating."

"It gave me a much deeper understanding of myself and other people."

Taster	Full Programme
Thursday, 11th July 2019 18.00 - 20.00 Islington Town Hall N1 2UD	**2 x Saturday daytimes plus 4 x Thursday evenings** Coming soon in September

Book your place and find out more:

@ http://talk-for-health.eventbrite.com/

@ Text or call 07826 148 461

Email: info@talkforhealth.co.uk

Images

pp. 2–3	Northern Line Information Book provided to driver operators
p. 20	Undated photo of Margaret Thatcher found in 'Images' box at Covent Garden Market Authority archive
p. 21	Photo by Clive Boursnell currently on display in Covent Garden Flower Market Café
p. 22	Found in 'Historical' box at Covent Garden Market Authority archive
p. 23	PPE requirements from Methods Statement FLO-N202-2360000-TRK-MST-00002, July 2018
pp. 40–41	Original photos from personal collection of King Frankie Sinatra
p. 42	Digital archive document provided by GMW Architects (now Scott Brownrigg)
p. 60	Original photo of The Divine David from personal collection of King Frankie Sinatra
p. 61	Section of page from Readers Wifes scrapbook
p. 62	Funeral programme from personal collection of King Frankie Sinatra
p. 80	Photo of Julian Hows and the woman who gave him her uniform, Robert Woodman collection, Bishopsgate Institute
p. 81	Photos from personal collections of Malc McDonald and Joe Brown
p. 82	Drawing from Transport for London Corporate Archives
p. 89	South London Press, 2 July 1976
p. 100	Miners ascending steps at Kennington shaft
p. 101	Mark Thompson inflates balloon for acoustic test
p. 102	Early 20th century drawing used by Tunnels Team, original in London Transport Museum archive
p. 120	Goshems Farm: The jetty and the Thames
p. 121	Goshems Farm: Northern line 'muck'
p. 122	Phases of land re-used at Goshems Farm
p. 123	Poster from London Transport Museum archive. A copy is stuck above Train Manager's desk at Golders Green
pp. 126–131	Found in 'Historical' box at Covent Garden Market Authority archive
pp. 132–133	Photo by David Curran, Flickr. © Creative Commons
p. 135	Found in Bishopsgate Institute
p. 136	Signage in 'station box', Battersea site, September 2019
p. 137	Poster at Camelford House, FLO Offices, September 2019
pp. 138–139	Islington Tribune, 21 June 2019

All other images taken by the artist on site at the Northern Line Extension, 2017–2019

151 152 153 154 155 156 157 158 159 160
161 162 163 164 165 166 167 168 169 170
171 172 173 174 175 176 177 178 179 180
181 182 183 184 185 186 187 188 189 190
191 192 193 194 195 196 197 198 199 200

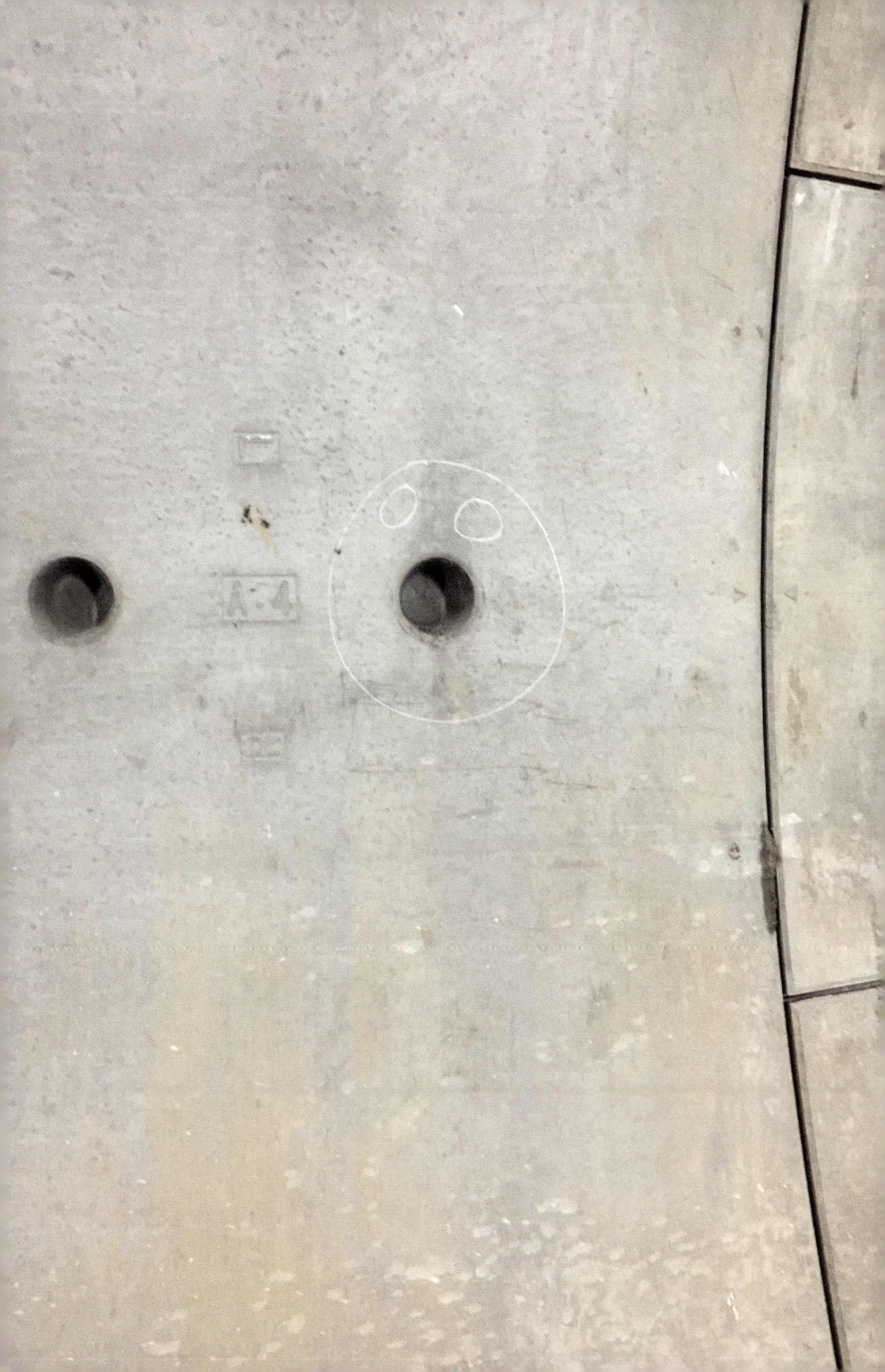
A-4

RV14 LZW
JCB
520-40
(IRISH)
BATTERSEA SCISSORS
PTS D4 XING X6
492A
424C
423C
424D
423C
424D

SWL5000KG

NGINEERS BOX

Our Pink Depot
The Gay Underground
FLO-N202-236000000-
TRK-MST-00002-SAY-
HELLO-WAVE-GOODBYE-
KEN-NIE-BPS
by Nina Wakeford

Published by Book Works in association with Art on the Underground
Distributed by Book Works

Book Works Co-Series No. 19

Commissioning Editor: Kiera Blakey
Copy editing and proofreading by Lizzie Homersham
Additional image research by Lydia Briggs
Designed by Fraser Muggeridge studio
Typeset in Arial, Pixel Arial, Bookmania, New Johnston, Garamond Megafont
Printed in Belgium

Book Works receives National Portfolio funding from Arts Council England. This project has been generously funded by Art on the Underground.

ISBN: 978 1 912570 06 5

Book Works
19 Holywell Row
London EC2A 4JB
bookworks.org.uk
+44 (0)20 7247 2203

Art on the Underground
Transport for London
197 Blackfriars Road
London SE1 8NJ
art.tfl.gov.uk
+44 (0)20 3054 8128

Enormous thanks to Kiera Blakey, Curator, Art on the Underground for making this project possible and always championing it without hesitation, and to Eleanor Pinfield for powers of advocacy with all the stakeholders, internal and external. Thanks also – on site at the Northern Line Extension and Kennington: Yorkshireman Mark Thompson and his Tunnels Team, Aleisha Young, Andres, Aniol Jolanta, Anna Hladkyi, Becky Richardson, Bethany Selwyn, Carl Painter, Christine Sutcliffe, Claire Taylor, Daniel Owens, John Davis, Jonathan Cooper, 'Juanjo', Liam Greaney, Louise Ellery, Mario Palma, Melanie Barker, Neil Watson, Paloma Rodicio, Pedram Mostaeddi, Tracey Culpan. From the Northern line stations: Alexander Garnett-Scherer (Golders Green) and his network of LGBT drivers, train managers, and station staff, especially those from Golders Green and Morden who participated in the Historic Trackwalk: Brendan Carey, Colin Anthony, Dave Bacon, John Krol, Leah Seabra Goncalves, Natalie Rhule. Other LGBT ex-drivers and guards: Joe Brown, Julian Hows. From OUTbound, TfL's LGBT+ staff network: Hannah Wood, Joe Brown, Kyle Monk, Malc McDonald. At Covent Garden Flower Market and the Market Authority: Alastair Owen, Bob from L. Mills, and all the salesmen (and Maurice), Cassie Burt, Clive Boursnell (photographer). For additional memories of the Market Tavern: the Duckie crew, in particular The Readers Wifes; John from Heavy Petal flowers, SE1; Fisch/King Frankie Sinatra, the Chain Reaction rebel dykes and their DJ friends in London and Brighton. At Goshems Farm: Maria Anton-Garcia. At the Royal College of Art: Hannah Lambert, Juan Cruz and the Research Office. At Fraser Muggeridge studio: Fraser, Joe Nava. At Book Works: Gavin Everall, Jane Rolo, Lizzie Homersham and Paul Sammut.

Research and production assistance: Adele Fletcher, Aliceson Carter, Cairo Clarke, Fiona Hale (translation), John Zammit, Joseph Noonan-Ganley, Kate Briggs, King Frankie Sinatra/Fisch, Martina Schmuecker, Paul Bavister, Sasha Roseneil, Stefan Dickers, Soundnode.

Art on the Underground would like to thank Cairo Clarke, FLO, Goshems Farm, Lambeth Council, Mark Thompson, Matt's Gallery, Nine Elms team at Wandsworth Council, OUTbound, and RCA Riverlight.

For image reproduction Art on the Underground and Book Works would like to thank: Bishopsgate Institute (Robert Woodman Archive), Clive Boursnell, Covent Garden Market Authority, Joe Brown, London Transport Museum, Malc McDonald, Scott Brownrigg, Transport for London. For song lyrics: Soft Cell.

BOO
KWO
RKS

ART ON THE UNDERGROUND

Supported using public funding by
ARTS COUNCIL ENGLAND